It Started
with
Pop-Tarts®...

An Alternative Approach
to Winning the Battle of Bulimia

It Started
with
Pop-Tarts®...

*An Alternative Approach
to Winning the Battle of Bulimia*

Lori Hanson

25379 Wayne Mills Pl. #228
Valencia, CA 91355
www.ShewolfPress.com

This book is intended as a general guide to the topics discussed. It is not intended and should not be used as a substitute for professional advice (medical, legal or otherwise) and the reader is advised to seek independent, professional advice.

Although every precaution has been taken to verify the accuracy of the information contained herein, the author and publisher assume no responsibility for any errors or omissions. No liability is assumed for damages that may result from the use of information contained herein. Additionally, this is a work in the nature of a memoir, not a work of journalism; the interchanges with the people portrayed herein are the recreation of the author's own emotions and memory.

It Started With Pop-Tarts... is not in any manner affiliated with, or sponsored or endorsed by the Kellogg Company, owner of the Pop-Tarts® trademark.

Pop-Tarts® is a registered trademark of the Kellogg Company and is used without its sponsorship or permission.

Barbie® is a registered trademark of Mattel, Inc., and is used without its sponsorship or permission.

Holosync® is a registered trademark of Centerpointe Research Institute and is used without its sponsorship or permission.

PUBLISHED BY: Shewolf Press
                 25379 Wayne Mills Pl. #228, Valencia, CA 91355
                 www.ShewolfPress.com

Cover design by F + P Graphic Design
Front cover illustration by Lace Hanson and Bobbi Shupe
Interior design by WESType Publishing Services, Inc., of Boulder, Colorado
Author Photo, Photos by Felicia

First Edition.

ISBN: 978-0-9800128-0-4

Printed and bound in the USA

   10 9 8 7 6 5 4 3 2 1 0

Books may be purchased in quantity and/or special sales by contacting the publisher, Shewolf Press, at 25379 Wayne Mills Pl. #228, Valencia, CA 91355, 661-670-0729 or through the website, ShewolfPress.com.

Table of Contents

Acknowledgements

Donna Cohen, thank you for being my sales mentor and friend during the short time you were in my life. You had such a positive impact and helped me believe I could achieve anything as a salesperson...and as a person. You were there when I needed advice and every time I changed jobs. And it was you who helped me to see it was time to do something different, which led to this book. You were truly an inspiration. I miss your laughter and boundless energy!

Anne Rojo—you were the beginning of my "alternative journey." You helped me feel safe stepping outside of the box. Thank you for sharing your soul so openly and understanding that I had a lot to learn. Your warmth and love for others radiates from your core and is a welcome change in this world!

Tina Meyer, thank you for all you gave to me through my healing. You are indeed a gift! You brought so much enlightenment to my life and helped me learn how to feel. You are an incredible, caring healer and friend.

Thanks to Shauna Sindo for all the expert advice, great acupuncture treatments and information you shared with me. You got me back on track and had a profound impact in my life.

Susanna Horton, through you I have found a great spiritual teacher and healer. Thank you for helping me to find the next level. With your guidance I was able to remove the training wheels and continue working on my own. You are a great source of inspiration.

Victoria Quintana, thanks for being supportive, caring and an enthusiastic cheerleader throughout my journey!

Judith Briles, thank you for seeing the potential in my project and for believing in it. You have been a great mentor and source of knowledge as I launched my career as an author. I couldn't have done it without you!

Barb Munson, thank you for your enthusiasm and expertise! Your editorial contributions, ideas and advice helped me elevate this book to the next level.

Thanks to Ronnie Moore for making this easy. Your experience and creativity in design made this a beautiful product.

Thanks to my parents Don and Rolene for bringing me into this world so I could experience this journey and find my path. You provided me with the tools I needed to be successful in life.

Thanks to my brother Don and my sisters, Cynthia, Debbi and Keri, for putting up with my crazy obsession all of these years. You have all been there at different times in my life to support and hold me up when I needed it.

To Henry, thanks for your patience, love and support through this journey. You brought so many new things to my world and for that I will be eternally grateful.

*This book is dedicated to all who fall prey to—
and get trapped in the pressure and expectations
of society to look perfect. May you find the true
meaning of life—beyond the mirror and enjoy it!*

Introduction

So, why me? Why does my story matter? You don't know me. I'm not a celebrity. I am only one of many women who spent years of their lives abusing food and alcohol as a substitute for feeling and dealing with emotions.

This is why: I am forty-eight years old and have battled with bulimia and my self-image for thirty-four years. I was haunted with hatred for myself and my body since I was fourteen. It was a long struggle, a very long fight.

Why, somewhere along the path, didn't someone help me learn how to *feel*? Why wasn't there help to figure out how to deal with and express my emotions? Why, once I finally stopped bingeing on food, hadn't I realized that all I was doing for the *next* ten years was trading it for alcohol? Something I didn't discover until I started to write this book!

So my path to healing has been a long one. And I didn't follow the typical clinical steps beyond my initial counseling in the mid '80s. I didn't go to "group" sessions and commiserate with other women who had eating disorders. I had to find my own way through this. What follows is my story, the events that shaped my very poor self-esteem, my reactions to those events, my beliefs, and my ultimate discovery of a *new* self.

My recovery has involved many steps, including improving my self-esteem; employing good nutrition, exercise and natural supplements; working with the subconscious and the law of intention to create the body I wanted; and using several forms of bodywork (Hellerwork, energy healing, acupuncture). These all helped me to heal (and I mean deeply!) the energy and beliefs that had been stored in my body for many years. Although very painful and difficult, I have faced these things in order to grow beyond them and become a healthy, "whole" human being.

Many of us grew up in dysfunctional homes; we grew up with poor self-esteem and grew into adults "with baggage." The result? The country now has a whole generation of parents with low self-esteem raising children with even less self-esteem. The evidence is everywhere. The high percentage of young children and teens who are overweight is astounding! The way children and teenagers treat each other with the "It's all about me" approach to life. This isn't how we were meant to live!

The very early years are when self-esteem is shaped in a child. That is when the change has to start. But to give our children strong self-esteem and a strong sense of self, the parents must first love themselves. This, I believe, is the core issue that begins to feed bulimia, anorexia and other similar forms of addiction, self abuse, compulsive and self-destructive behaviors.

Eating disorders in America have reached epidemic levels:

✧ 7 million women have them.
✧ 1 million men and children from all segments of society are affected.
✧ 86% report the onset of illness by age twenty.
✧ 77% report the duration of illness from one to fifteen years.
✧ 6% of serious cases die.
✧ Only 50% report being cured.[1]

Treatment costs U.S. businesses approximately $4 billion a year.[2] And since individual treatment can easily cost $30,000 a month for inpatient care, to $100,000 for outpatient treatment[3], this is a monumental problem for everybody.

I am writing this book to share with you what I have learned, in the hope that I can save you from wasting as many years of your life as I did *obsessed* with how I looked. My goal is to help you get beyond starting each day by looking in the mirror at your body to decide if it is a good or bad day. To inspire you to find help and healing in your life *now* so you can enjoy life as a normal, healthy person, a person who is balanced, loves yourself and sees the value of what you brings to this life. Free of the chains and bondage of food, alcohol or drug abuse as a substitute for feeling. Free to live and love life to its fullest potential!

—Lori Hanson

PART ONE

Chapter One

⌘

My Life

It's almost midnight. I'm sitting on the couch, drowsy after yet another food-induced stupor. I have to work tomorrow and I can hardly breathe, I ate so much. There's no way I will be able to sleep tonight.

This is SO stupid! I did it again. What the hell is wrong with me!

The pressure of the day once again drove me to my place of personal solace. Well, actually it's more of a personal numbness, but it's the place I run to when...

✧ Life gets too hard
✧ I'm lonely
✧ I'm upset
✧ I'm frustrated
✧ I need answers I don't have
✧ I'm angry
✧ I feel left out

✧ My body looks and feels like crap
✧ I want to scream
✧ I want to cry
✧ I don't want to feel!

It's a vicious cycle, and one I learned to perform with honors.

Tonight? A large four-cheese pizza, with bread sticks; a half bag of nachos; a half-gallon of Baskin-Robbins Pralines 'n Cream ice cream; and half a bag of Oreos.

Dammit! I was just getting myself back on track and feeling better, and here I am again. Why do I do this? Why can't I control it? Why is there no way to stop myself from the frenzied need to eat until I can't move? I hate myself! I'm so miserable I could scream. Tomorrow I will be all swollen; my suit will be tight. Oh shit, I forgot! I have to make a presentation in a meeting tomorrow. Everyone will notice. They will all see how big my stomach looks. I will be so embarrassed and mortified—yet again.

I push myself up from the couch and collapse into bed. Finding a comfortable position where I can fall sleep is impossible. My stomach hurts *so* bad. I'm so full, I can't believe I'm here again. Tomorrow will be a chore, because I won't get much sleep due to "carb overload."

It's morning. I hear the alarm clock. I'm so groggy that it's all I can to do to coax myself out of bed.

I'm going to be late! I don't want to move. I don't want to get dressed. I want to hibernate. I can't possibly face the world outside today. That's it... tonight when I come home, I will eat healthy. No more sweets! I'll throw the rest of the Oreos out on my way to work.

❧ ❧ ❧

Three weeks have passed. It's time to weigh and measure like I do *every* month. I have made some progress since my last slide. My clothes are starting to feel looser and I feel my energy starting to return. It's been a good couple of weeks and this time I think I'm on track. I can win this battle. The next time I get upset I just won't eat, I promise; I will be strong. I won't let food get the better of me.

Hurray! I lost 3 pounds since last month, not bad considering the last backslide. (The last binge went on for an entire week—I bought more Oreos and ice cream on the way home and another large bag of Nachos and ended up fixated on sweets for the next five days.)

Well, let me back up and tell you how it all started. I was an early inductee into the sugar "hall of fame." There was always ice cream with homemade hot fudge sauce for special occasions and we *always* ate two bowls. (The memory of stirring it into a thick "milk shake" in my bowl still makes me smile!)

Food was associated with family celebrations, social get-togethers, Saturday nights spent at friends' homes and holidays. Food was *central* to life. I grew up vegetarian with lots of cheese and dairy (I've since become a vegan and don't eat meat or dairy).

Many childhood issues helped form a self-destructive behavior. As I reached the adolescent years, my interest in boys, combined with a poor self-image, unacceptable body and lack of faith in myself, sent me to the safe haven of bulimia. Although I had no idea what it was at the time.

My bulimia was at its worst during college and the first few years of my career. By that time, it was a chronic cycle of bingeing to excess, followed by religious dieting and starving myself for weeks to compensate. I was never able to make myself throw up, which in hindsight was probably a good thing; my teeth are still strong. The thought of using laxatives to purge, which a friend told me she did, was unthinkable to me.

So I rode the proverbial seesaw and followed the ups and downs of my weight, a perfect yo-yo cycle. I would lose 10 pounds over a two- or three-month period, and gain it all back in a week. I weighed and measured religiously, it gave me a regular way to chastise myself for screwing up or feeling like I was making progress when I wasn't in "binge mode."

Most people's first reaction when they hear I was bulimic for so long assume I purged by throwing up, but as noted by Dr. Sacker in his book *Regaining Your Self*, bulimia has two types—purging and non-purging.[1]

By the mid-80s I had several well-developed "binge foods" (foods that triggered a binge). If I could keep away from sweets and not eat candy or chocolate, I was fine. If I took that first bite, it would often send me into a five-day sugar feeding frenzy. It was typically a week before I could stop the cycle and get control of myself again.

One binge favorite—which I couldn't keep in the house—was good ole Kraft Macaroni & Cheese. (You have to buy the deluxe family size or two of the small ones in order to reach true gluttony.)

Fettuccini Alfredo was another creamy, fat, comforting, sluggish binge food that I inhaled when life got really tough! You get the idea. Over the years, there were things I couldn't have around if I wanted to remain on track. But in the event of a trauma, sadness, loneliness or disappointment—I just went to the store whatever time of the day or night and got my fix. When the going got tough, I ran for cover into the state of numbness I could create with food. Plus, when it was all said and done, I could totally berate myself for being *so stupid* once again—an incredibly vicious cycle.

As a person who abuses food, you do so many embarrassing things. Things you never tell another person about. If there was a man in my life, which in the worst years there typically wasn't—I always found a place to binge alone. This isn't something you do in front of another person. And it isn't about the food. Hell, I never tasted it going down because I was shoveling it in so fast!

All I wanted was to feel a distance from the world, to achieve the state of numb where I didn't care about anyone or anything, not even myself. After all, why did I deserve any praise? I was just a huge screw up! I couldn't control my food intake, I didn't look like other women whom I thought were attractive; and I certainly didn't look like the tall, thin women with big boobs (a k a Barbie® doll figures) that most of the men I knew went for. I had curves, which were made increasingly worse (in my eyes) by bingeing.

Mind you, I'm 5'1" and in those days my weight typically fluctuated between 118 and 125 pounds. The most I ever weighed was 140 and that was because of a bet I made with my sister as I headed into my divorce. The bet was that I could skyrocket from 130 to 140 pounds by Christmas, and I did. Sadly it was mostly from alcohol.

I tried to join Weight Watchers once when I weighed 118. People there thought I was nuts. They didn't think I was overweight, but I was heavier than I felt I should be. I tried lots of diets, had loads of determination, did my Jane Fonda workouts (go for the burn!), and Jackie Sorenson Aerobics classes—but never really made any progress.

I hated the way I looked, and wanted so much to be thin. I didn't like my curves or pooch belly and wanted to look like all the Barbie dolls that were constantly thrown in my face from the media. After all, that's what men wanted, right?

The Early Years

I was always independent, from as early as I can remember. I had two older sisters who always picked on me. By early grade school one would punch me in the stomach, the other stood there and laughed. I didn't really feel like I fit in or was wanted as part of the trio. So I typically played alone, and enjoyed it. From the age of three, I was begging for a truck to play with. I wasn't into dolls, and never wanted or had a Barbie. (Interesting, huh?) I liked my individuality!

There were always so many things to measure up to—which I *never* felt I did. Mom was a total perfectionist and was into her career as a musician. I was a necessary evil as a result of the fact that she loved babies. Unfortunately for her, or for me, the babies (my sisters and I) didn't disappear as we grew older and we required love, attention and affection.

Some of my earliest memories involve days in which we had to adjust to her work schedule. I had many baby sitters in those days—whomever Mom knew that was available. We lived in Cedar Lake, Michigan at the time. My parents worked at an academy (a Seventh-Day Adventist parochial boarding school, grades 9-12). I was raised Seventh-Day Adventist.

My dad was the accountant for the academy. Mom was in charge of the music program. All this meant to me at the age of four was that Mom was always busy with the students. If she wasn't directing choir, she was giving piano, voice or organ lessons. All of the choir practices and performances kept her busy and unavailable from me most of the time. I got the message loud and clear: adapt to her schedule, or go without. So I adapted the best I could.

Mom told me numerous stories about my antics when she was at choir practice. I used to stand behind her and direct, like "Minnie me" (a miniature of her). She turned around to discover this when the choir burst out laughing.

I also "adapted" by falling madly in love with Dan (a sophomore). I was four. He carried me everywhere in his arms. When the choir was at our house for lunch after church, I performed, which included doing summersaults in my church dress. I took note of and learned early how to give a great performance by clowning to get my share of attention. I *knew* how to entertain the entire group and make people laugh.

One of the earliest "big" disappointments was when I was about five. Mom told me I could pack a lunch and come to the gym the next day to meet her for lunch. I was *so* excited! When I woke the next morning, my throat was bothering me and it was hard to swallow. Mom was looking at me kind of funny. Then she told me I had the mumps and would have to stay home.

I was heart broken; my big lunch date with Mom was cancelled. I was sure she would stay home and take care of me—but she had to go to work. I was crushed! Nothing ever got in the way of her work. Why did she have to give so much to those kids anyway? And why did she always seem to have so many "favorites" who took her away from us? It was as if we (her kids) just weren't good enough. This pattern continued throughout grade school.

We had moved several times and now lived outside Columbus, Ohio on five and a half acres. That was awesome—but our ride home from school was with whomever had a music lesson that day. If no one had a music lesson, we walked about a mile to the hospital where my dad worked and waited until he was ready to go home.

Some days this was a complete drag, but I loved hanging out with my dad, he seemed so smart to me. He was a hospital administrator for a private psychiatric hospital. He worked with doctors and ran all of these meetings, and was so organized.

Everyone at the hospital was friendly. Dad's secretary was always fun and talked with me for a while if she wasn't too busy. At the end of the day, Dad would tell me about the events of his day and what his meetings were about, what was cooking and what problems he was trying to solve. I loved that!

Just as we were settling into our new house and community, my mom had another baby, a boy; I was ten. Mom told me early on I was supposed to be a boy (Brent David was the name they had picked out). Alas, I was a disappointment, the third girl. They were so thrilled to finally have their boy.

It was obvious after Don Junior's arrival that the sun rose and set on my little brother. I was nominated the quintessential "built in" babysitter. So as Mom had music lessons to teach, and my brother had colic on a regular basis, *I* paced the floor with him. To make matters worse, Mom kept insisting that I had begged for another baby and regularly implied that it was my fault he was here. Hell, I didn't have anything to do with his conception!

I can still hear her telling everyone, "Well, Lori just loves babies, she begged for us to have another one," followed by me saying, "Mom, I did not!"

And so the development of my role in the family evolved. I'd gone from being the "baby" (and *never* really feeling "babied") to being the middle child, which then morphed into the role of oldest of the "second family." Mom had yet another baby when I was fourteen. Initially, I was very close with my little sister Keri. She was my shadow, loved hanging out with me and was quite the ham herself. But at fourteen I headed off to boarding school so I only saw her once a month.

Things had evolved to such a point of control by

my mother that I couldn't wait to get away from her and live on my own in a dorm. But I'm getting ahead of myself.

The Sickly Child

From a very early age, I always had something medically wrong with me. I was the sickly child or so I had been told repeatedly. My tonsils were removed at the age of three to improve my hearing. My older sister Cindy and I went in together and my uncle performed the surgery on both of us. I recently asked my mom what had prompted them to do this, how they knew I had a hearing problem, and she couldn't remember. I did some research and found a lot of "they just did this back then." Now they know better since tonsils have a lot to do with your immune system.

The surgery didn't help my hearing; at age four they put tubes in my ears. When that didn't help, they sent me in for allergy tests. The tests suggested my hearing would improve if I didn't use milk. So when I was eight they took me off milk for two years... it made no improvement in my hearing. And then I had to learn to like milk again. During my hiatus Mom bought Coffee Rich for me to use with cereal and it was way different than milk! At ten they put tubes in my ears again. I went in for weekly allergy shots, took allergy pills daily and, to my recollection, none of this helped.

I also had been through several bouts of ear infections. Back then they gave me straight penicillin as an antibiotic. Around age twelve in 1972, when I got an ear infection again, the doctor was concerned about the amount and frequency of penicillin I had taken (something that would come back to haunt me in later years). As I understood it your body can build up a tolerance to penicillin. If at some point in life you had a severe type of infection and needed the full strength penicillin—it would have no effect.

I was given several audiology tests that confirmed that I had a hearing loss in my right ear. But nothing made my hearing any better. I hated being seen as the "sickly child," I never really felt sick and they couldn't ever diagnose *anything* that I was allergic to. I was tired of it already.

By high school, they had me on Dimetapp, a children's allergy formula. Living in a dormitory, away from home and experiencing freedom, I learned that several pills taken together actually produced a fun little "high." I couldn't believe Mom never caught on why my allergy pills needed to be refilled so frequently.

I continued to get ear infections. In my senior year of high school and freshman year of college I had seven ear infections, within a year and a half!

I learned to adjust to life with my "bad ear" and poor hearing. There were times when having a bad ear was useful, living in a noisy dorm, and later when I traveled every week and lived in hotels while I was a consultant. You can block out a lot of noise!

So this sickly early child development continued the thought in "little Lori" that I wasn't quite right. I definitely wasn't perfect and I didn't fit the "norm."

To this day, I struggle with this belief and often fight the notion of being sickly. I never could understand why they singled me out and made my health such an issue. I wasn't overtly aware of my hearing issues and for all the tests and experiments, nothing helped, so it must not have been that big of a problem!

⍺ ⍺ ⍺

During late grade school and early high school years I watched my mother struggle with depression. She went to counseling for years and took medications that strung her out. She told me her mother had had some mental health issues and apparently this ran in the family. I *knew* I wanted to avoid that at all costs. I was going to be very mentally and physically healthy! I was going to find my own path and do what felt right to me—when I was old enough. I wanted to do something athletic, maybe be a professional tennis player like Chris Evert—but there was never any parental encouragement or support for me to pursue these feelings. I was guided, instead, toward music.

"Little Lori" — Kindergarten

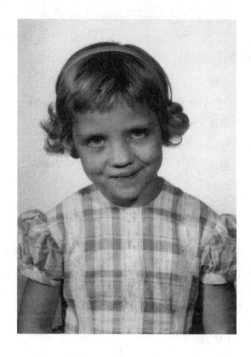

I was intense—even as a kid!

Chapter Two

Issues Evolve

My self-image started eroding in fourth grade. I was *so* self-conscious because I didn't feel I measured up anywhere. I'll explain more about why in a minute. My oldest sister Cindy ran away from home the first time when she was fourteen. I watched the chain of events unfold and told myself I wouldn't follow that path because she got her butt beat with a belt when they found her and brought her home.

In my book, Cindy was the consummate black sheep of the family. Always pushing the limits, always in trouble, and I couldn't quite make the connection of what it was doing for her. She just seemed to thrive on bucking authority.

Sister #2, Debbi, was more of an issue for me. She was the epitome of the "golden child," complete with halo. She made straight A's, played the piano by ear (which I couldn't do), was on the gymnastics team (I never made it) and always seemed to be in "favorite" zone. In addition, she regularly felt the need to tell on Cindy and me. Had I ever had children, I would not have had three!

Debbi was Miss Goody Two Shoes and I could not stand her. She was always telling me what to do and in general taking advantage of the fact that she was older.

By the time I hit the ripe old age of eleven, Cindy had turned me on to smoking cigarettes (Kools, of course, this was the early '70s). This was followed in eighth grade by the introduction of smoking pot and drinking Strawberry Boones Farm. The *big* deal back in those days was listening to *rock* music when my parents weren't home. Mom, being the classically trained musician, could *not* deal with the evolution of rock. The family joke is that Cindy brought home a 45 rpm record of The Letterman's "Born Free" and Mom broke it! (She has since grown in her musical tastes, but still no rock music.)

A few times when we were listening to rock Debbi ratted on us—if she thought she was going to get caught. Any time the risk got above a certain level, she caved and pointed the finger at us. I observed this behavior and decided I wasn't going to replicate it either.

The good thing about having two older siblings— if you're smart—you have someone to observe and learn from. There were a number of things I watched them get in trouble for and knew I wasn't going down that path, although I found a few of my own.

Ohio

While all this was evolving, my parents, the nomads, continued to move every four years or so. I was born in Saginaw, Michigan; we lived in Detroit when I was two; moved to Cedar Lake by age three; spent one summer in Berrien Springs, Michigan and then moved to Hinsdale, Illinois by age six, just in time for first grade.

We landed just outside Columbus, Ohio as I started fourth grade. The move to Columbus was a traumatic one. I loved my school and friends in Hinsdale. However, Mom had started the "Your friends are not acceptable" speeches about my best friend in first grade. From then on, anyone that I chose as a friend wasn't the "right type" of friend to have, they were "bad influences" on me and I was restricted from being friends with them. Well, screw that! They became my *best* friend. After years of Mom's rejection due to her work, followed by a phase where nothing I did was acceptable, I was out to do anything she told me *not* to. Yeah, I was a rebellious little thing, and sometimes still am!

So I left a school with twenty classmates in third grade and found myself in a fourth grade class with six other kids...all of whom had been together the first three years. I was the intruder! These guys were not thrilled that I was there, didn't accept me and served up my first experience of "cliques."

The girls were snots and would only interact with me on days they were at odds with their "best friends." There was one boy in the class who I got along with after a while. He was a good 75 pounds overweight so no one really accepted him. As if this wasn't enough, my brother arrived and I've got baby-sitter duty *all* the time. I hated Ohio.

I remember sitting on the hamper in my parent's bathroom while mom got dressed (I don't remember getting her undivided attention unless I was in trouble), telling her why each and every kid there hated me and would not give me the time of day. I finally found a new friend in the fifth grade, a year ahead of me, we were like two peas in the pod—until Mom found out. And then I was told I couldn't be friends with her. Grrr! This continued throughout grade school.

I loved playing with boys and playing sports like flag football and baseball, and I earned the Presidential Award each year from fifth to eighth grade. My breasts developed in fourth grade, earlier than the other girls, and two boys in my sister Deb's class called me "28 Triple A" when I would walk by. I was embarrassed, yet I loved the attention. I actually was crazy about boys, starting in kindergarten, and was always looking for their acceptance and attention. I even went steady for three days in third grade with the boy across the street…then he broke up with me and broke my heart!

Shortly after we moved to Ohio I got letters from a boy back in Hinsdale whom I had *really* liked— man, I hated that we had moved.

I'll never forget getting busted for kissing a boy during recess when I was in fourth grade. Only four of us were outside for recess that day because it was cold...my friend Kim, and Jeff and Randy, who were all third graders. We were just hanging out on the swings and dared each other to kiss. I guess my teacher looked out the window to check on us and caught the smooch. She sent me home to ask my parents what they thought of me kissing a boy. I told her my parents were okay with it! Ask a stupid question...

I had several boyfriends older than I was and ones that my mother didn't approve of (big surprise). I went steady and hid the rings or bracelets they gave me. When I was twelve, I started to fool around and experiment some with second and third base. We had an organization in our church—the equivalent of boy scouts and girl scouts that was co-ed (Pathfinders). We learned crafts (like how to tie knots) and went on co-ed camping trips. It appeared my mom had en- listed spies to keep an eye on me when I wasn't at home. One spy reported me for being behind the gym making out with my heart throb from seventh grade. I couldn't get away with anything! But more impor- tantly, I didn't feel I could breathe.

Middle School Years

By seventh grade I was an accomplished violinist by choice, a pianist by duress (Mom's choice), and a saxophone player in school band because Dad played sax growing up. I also sang regularly at church. But I wanted to play more tennis!

With all the music, I was spread too thin and found convenient ways to skip practicing some days. If I missed *any* of my practice sessions during the week, though, I had to spend all day Sunday making up every half hour I'd missed on piano *and* violin. This didn't endear my mom to me in the least.

I couldn't have any posters or a radio in my room (Donny Osmond, Michael Jackson and David Cassidy pictures were all hidden on the back of my bedroom door!) and I couldn't wear short skirts like other girls. I felt like a freak! I hated Mom's overly protective nature, conservatism, religious beliefs and control. I was *miserable*.

My relationships with schoolmates had eroded so badly by the eighth grade I asked my parents if I could transfer to public school. To my shock they said yes. So I transferred to a middle school—whoa! This was a much bigger school. They had lockers, I got to go to different classrooms for my classes and there were *so many* cute guys.

Yeah, well, I had glasses and braces, was a bit

insecure and not very outgoing. Although I loved the change, I was intimidated by my new school. For whatever reason several of the guys from band started to call me "Dogface" and would bark when they saw me coming down the hallway. Charming! I *knew* I wasn't that ugly. It's amazing to me that any of us grow up through the formative years with kids being as mean and spiteful as they are!

I did make a couple of friends at public school, but the whole experience was more painful than at church school. So, after just eight weeks, I went back to church school and finished eighth grade there. No one welcomed me back, there was no love fest…but I felt like I didn't fit in anywhere.

Dad

My father was always my role model. I was in awe of him but he was somewhat disengaged at home. He would teach me about T-accounts and accounting on our drives to and from work and school. I thought he was so intelligent, running a hospital, meeting with the Board and managing his investments. When I started my career, I was going to be a hospital president—just like him!

I was often frustrated that Dad wouldn't stand up to my mom and would back her on stuff that I didn't believe he really agreed with; he just didn't want to cross her. The way Mom explained it...he made executive decisions all day and didn't want to make decisions when he got home.

Mind you, he wasn't perfect in my eyes; there were times when he could be incredibly frustrating too. Typically when any one of us would ask him if we could do something or go somewhere, for the longest time he wouldn't answer. And then you would have to ask two or three more times to finally get an answer.

He called me "lardo" a few times. That really hurt my feelings. I had a little pooch belly then, but I was far from fat. In fact, in grade school I didn't have a weight problem.

Overall, though, I seemed to connect with my dad better than my sisters did because I thought I understood his perspective and was interested in the world of business. Looking back I may not have understood him as well as I thought I did, but it felt good at the time.

Grade School Years

First Grade

Sixth Grade

I notice in most of my childhood pictures from grade school I'm not smiling. I don't look like the "happy-go-lucky" child, and always have that deep intensity in my eyes.

Chapter 3

❧

Bulimia Begins: High School

I finished grade school and at fourteen was ready to start my freshman year of high school. I left home for boarding school in Mt. Vernon, Ohio. Freedom from the controlling grip of my mother, freedom from her lectures, her family worships, her disapproval and religious antics (more later)! I couldn't breathe around her. There was too much pressure and friction because of religious beliefs, a zillion restrictions and rules of what we could and could not do and so much judgment.

But, ironically, I could wear my skirts shorter at boarding school than I could at home. Mom didn't know whom I hung out with and couldn't be there to judge my every move. This was going to be a blast!

Alas, there were plenty of faculty members now who were watching my every move like a hawk. Had she warned them?

Since this was a parochial school, we had to take

classes in religion and attend church programs and worships that were mandatory. Of course, my best girlfriend was "unacceptable" and, even though I was at boarding school, my mother told me to stay away from her. Yeah, right!

I became a bit more rebellious as I got some freedom. But I didn't feel accepted by most of the other kids (I wasn't cool enough) and went through three roommates in my first year. I even dated a few guys and soon was having fun with the few friends I had.

My older sister was a senior at Mt. Vernon during my first year there and was on an ego trip. She had this attitude that seniors were so much better than freshmen. Whatever! Even her friends treated me like I was a lowly creature.

I liken this period to being a ball in a pinball machine. I was bouncing off the walls and didn't feel stable anywhere. I was out to find my independence and my motto was "Rules are made to be broken." I got involved in a number of things that weren't my brightest moves in life. But overall, I just didn't feel accepted. I wasn't one of the cool kids. *They* never gave me the time of day.

I started to eat out of frustration. This was the first time in my life I had "real" supper prepared and I fully enjoyed it. I gained 14 pounds in the first six weeks I was there. Although my mom was a great cook she was usually teaching a music lesson at dinner time so it was typically "fend for yourself."

The food at school was so unhealthy! Macaroni and cheese, lasagna, Tater Tots, all kinds of fried vegetarian foods and entrees loaded with cheese and calories. Oh, yeah, and big, wonderful fresh-made cinnamon rolls on Saturday mornings. Yum!

First Diet

I quickly learned that, to control my weight, I was going to have to go on a "diet" and skip suppers. This is what I saw other girls doing and it seemed to work for them. I did it for a while, but when I got frustrated, all I wanted was to eat.

My Undoing

One day a girlfriend and I stole an industrial-size bag of Frosted Pop-Tarts® Brown Sugar Cinnamon toaster pastries from the cafeteria and hid them in my dorm room. We had a regular "quick snack," and I had my first official stash of sugar to binge on.

Before this I had never had any issues with my weight. Now I was embarrassed because my butt and legs were the first to go (or grow). Suddenly I had "thunder thighs."

It was shortly after this that food became the substitute for dealing with emotion. I didn't realize it at the time, and didn't fully understand it until many years later. When I got upset, I ate. When I was frustrated, I ate. When I was anxious or nervous, I ate. When I was happy and wanted to celebrate—you guessed it. All I wanted was ice cream, macaroni and cheese, or pizza. I craved food.

☞ ☞ ☞

I constantly had an overwhelming feeling that I just didn't fit in—*anywhere*. This translated into me being even more boy-crazy, looking for that attention and acceptance that was so lacking in my life. I dated a lot, but no one for very long. Some guys really liked me and I quickly tired of them. Other guys I really liked either didn't give me the time of day or I very quickly pushed them away.

My need to push the system grew. Boarding school began to feel like a prison camp to me—always someone watching, always someone waiting to get me in trouble! Why couldn't I be free? Why couldn't the adults just leave me alone! Early adolescence at its finest!

Getting Expelled from Boarding School

Then one day I pushed a little too hard. A new guy came to school mid-term. He was gorgeous and a rebel. My best friend Sue and I both liked him. Sue had to go away for the weekend to visit her grandparents. The new guy asked me to come sneak out with him and two other friends to smoke a cigarette on Saturday night while everyone else was at the Disney movie in the school gym. He asked me out! I was so smitten with him and really lost my senses.

Long graphic story short, we ended up staying out all night hiding from the school posse, who at one point were right outside the building we were in. We all got expelled. And now my friend Sue was sure to be mad at me on top of it.

Mom was furious. Facing my dad was no fun either; I hated always feeling like I had let him down. The school had a meeting to investigate what happened and determine our fate and Mom wouldn't even let me go. That really made me angry; I was supposed to be at that meeting. It was a miserable finale to a very unsettled school year. I ended up back in the middle school I had attended in eighth grade. (Except this time they weren't quite so mean.)

Work

I started working for my dad at thirteen. I helped him manage the books for a client who owned several properties and rented the homes. The summers during high school were spent working at my dad's psychiatric hospital. I started in the cafeteria, and then spent one summer in housekeeping. After learning how to type and because I was so fast I got to do medical secretarial work, filling in for secretaries while they went on vacation.

Most of the people at the hospital hated my sisters and me because we were the president's kids. I decided early on that I was not going to ride on my father's coattails—anything I did would be on my own.

Something interesting started to happen. Several of the men who worked around the hospital started to notice me. They were all much older than I was and I loved the flirting and attention. Here I was sixteen, kissing a construction worker who wore a wedding band. It gave me such a rush, being so "bad."

Another guy from the maintenance department was always flirting with me. We had lunch together on the lawn a couple of times, but it never amounted to more than fun conversation and flirtatious laughs. Somehow the acceptance from the older married men helped me to forget how the guys my age treated me. None of the guys I really liked gave me a second look.

Boarding School Round Two

I ended up back at Mt. Vernon for my sophomore year. At school our schedule was split days, half in classes and half working to help pay our school bills. Work came easy to me. I enjoyed it and found that it was easy to do more than what was asked. I ended up always working circles around other people. This became the *one* area where I shined and I felt like I measured up. I started to form close relationships with people who I worked with who were older than I, usually ten to fifteen years or more. That helped to fill the void due to lack of acceptance I felt from kids my age.

While at Mt. Vernon I played saxophone in the band, sang in the choir, and was often asked to sing for worships and sometimes church. I loved performing. When I sang I got lots of kudos and compliments. I was acknowledged for having a great voice. I still had a great sense of humor. I was always joking around in class and making other people laugh. The ham born as a youngster was still alive and well. I was quick with the humorous responses and was usually upbeat in spite of the emotional roller coaster. I just wanted to have fun.

My sophomore year I made some great guy friends who happened to be black (this was '75-'76). These guys were so totally accepting of me, they actually loved the way I looked, told me so regularly and made me feel like a million bucks—*and* they weren't looking for a Barbie girl. We hung out a lot, talked, laughed, flirted and joked around. They were great friends and not judgmental. I often sat with my new friends on the "other side" of the cafeteria where all the black kids sat, but all I did was make enemies of all the Sistas. This was not "acceptable" at this school so needless to say I was all over it in my rebellious state.

There was one guy, Henry, I *really* liked. I still remember the first day I saw him. I melted, he was so fine! Oh, I had it bad for him! But it just wasn't acceptable or appropriate for us to date. So we dated other people and found ways to talk and hang out. We did manage to find a secret place to sneak in a kiss without getting caught. But as usual someone told my parents about my new friends and they told me this had to stop.

My junior year, I got suspended the third week of school for smoking pot with a couple of friends in the dorm. We were so stoned we put the fan in the window backwards! While we were suspended we had to write a three-thousand-word essay. I wrote mine on the effects of marijuana. I detailed how the effect of marijuana was nothing like hallucinogenic drugs or heroin. Did I mention I was rebellious? I returned to prison camp after the suspension and was *miserable*. I decided to leave in the middle of the school year and finish at public school.

But I went back to Mt. Vernon on weekends as often as I could to visit Sue (we had remained friends). We would drink, smoke and find cute guys in town to hang out with. We also used to sneak into the boys dorm to see Henry and Sue's boy-toy. We had a blast. I missed her a lot, but could not deal with that school.

Public School

Public high school was nothing short of uneventful. All the kids had been together since first grade and I wasn't part of that bond. I didn't get the whole cheerleader thing and sure didn't feel like I looked as good as they did. Once again I just didn't fit in. I really didn't belong.

In the afternoons, I worked at the hospital in the Medical Records Department. The three older women I worked with took me under their wing and loved my warped sense of humor. Work was great! Their boss was a much younger guy who was a total dork. We formed a great female bond and ignored him as much as possible.

The need to act out when I got upset was still there. For a while I tried smoking cigarettes when I got upset. I wouldn't smoke the whole pack, and never started any regular smoking habits. It was just something I did when I got mad, frustrated or couldn't deal.

One night, I didn't air out the car very well and for some reason didn't pull it into the garage. When my dad came inside from putting the car away he confronted me about the smell of smoke in the car. I told him I was smoking, but only bought them when I got upset. He suggested in the future that I go to the mall, or go for a drive when I was upset and needed to blow off steam. This didn't turn out to be his best advice!

I discovered a place called Elaine Powers, where I started to work out in an attempt to get myself back into shape. I rode bike and jogged too (which I hated) because these were things Dad did and I thought they would help me regain my pre-boarding school figure.

The relationship with my mother continued to be incredibly strained. I was happier being at home where I had the freedom to drive to school and interact with more normal people than at prison camp. But the constant feeling that a noose was around my neck cutting off my air supply was always there.

I didn't want to be the person she wanted me to be, and all of her lectures, letters and mandatory worships did nothing more than push me even further away. I was filled with resentment and hatred toward her. I was *never* good enough, my friends were *never* acceptable and I was simply a "bad kid." Well I personally didn't think I was *that* bad.

In her effort to control the family my mother at times resorted to being a complete martyr; (in my eyes) she was so needy. She pushed my father away—never getting what she really wanted from him. She began to complain to me about things in their relationship that I really didn't want to know about. I didn't have my mother's perspective of the world and never understood why she would take the risk of complaining to me about my father—he was my role model!

There weren't a lot of happy memories for me my senior year of high school. I was often depressed, or lethargic from "carbing out" or now drinking. There were several times I was late for school because

I had diarrhea so bad I couldn't leave the house. (I recently found out this was the start of long-term bacterial imbalance.)

         ᏂᏂᏂ

    I finished high school and graduated. I was headed for yet another SDA school for college, which was the only way my parents would help me pay for it. I wasn't stupid! I knew I needed a college education to do what I wanted in life. But it was a means to an end. I wasn't a great student and sure wasn't ready for more religion.

    Looking back this probably was a good choice. Had I gone to a state school or university I may never have graduated as I was already drinking heavily. I was completely trashed at my high school graduation.

High School

Sophomore

My first weight gain and introduction to "thunder thighs" and being overweight by 10-15 pounds. At least here you can see signs of life and the mischievous Little Lori shines through!

Senior

This shot is from my senior year. I'm wearing the dress I made for my eighth grade graduation.

Mom finally *let me get wire framed glasses.* This was shortly after my first liquid diet where I got down to 110 pounds. I was about 112 here.

Chapter 4

❦

The Chronic Bulimia Years: College

Why I chose to go to college in Chattanooga, Tennessee is beyond me. No offense to those in Tennessee, but I'm a strong midwestern girl and I didn't fit in down in the South. I couldn't believe all the girls there were working on what I called their M.R.S. degrees. I was an accounting major.

The first year studies were fairly easy for me. I went through several roommates again continuing my pattern of dorm life. I was back in pinball mode. There were days I would decide to say "Hello" to all the other students I passed on the sidewalk. When they ignored me, I wondered what I had done, or what was wrong with me. I was *trying* to be outgoing! (This was my attempt to overcome being shy.)

By the time I started college I had learned to take out *all* my frustrations on food. Now it was related to how a guy treated me or whether one asked me out or not. I had such a strong need for acceptance. One night, *right* after eating dinner in the cafeteria, a guy who I was gaga about called and canceled a date for later that week. I was crushed! I marched right down to the snack bar and ordered a large pizza. After eating the whole thing, I followed it with as much ice cream as I could get down.

Poor me! How could he reject me that way? Didn't he know that his rejection had just knocked me down several more notches in "not being good enough?"

Over a couple of months I continued my pattern of dieting to get the weight off, measuring and weighing regularly. This was followed by getting upset and gaining back the full 10 pounds in less than a week. If I ate too much and made myself miserable, that was the price I had to pay for being so stupid yet again.

Part of the vicious cycle I had created myself. Sweets were dangerous for me—if I started, I couldn't stop. For a solid week I binged on Snickers bars, ice cream, cookies and M&Ms. If I stayed away from sweets I was okay. But if I got upset, hide the sugar!

I always marveled at the Barbie girls at college who enjoyed an ice cream bar after dinner and never seemed to gain an ounce. It just wasn't fair! Why couldn't *I* be like that? Once again all the guys seemed to be dating the Barbie girls, not girls like me who had curves in their hips.

During a call home to my dad, I mentioned something about gaining so much weight so quickly. He was very concerned about my behavior and told me how unhealthy it was for my body. I had a sense of that, but *no* control over it. I had no way to identify what I was feeling and express or experience it. I was just trying to find something or someone who would really love, accept and want me. I wasn't remotely interested in getting married. I was preparing for my career as a hospital president, just like Dad.

My first year at this college was a trip. I played in both the orchestra and band. Somehow, in all the commotion of being in the new school and all the religious pressure, I felt compelled—actually because of I guy I *really* liked—to give religion one more try.

I prayed, I got up early and did morning Bible studies and even broke every "evil" rock album I had, in an effort to be acceptable to God. How I lived to regret that move—breaking all my albums! I think that was also prompted by the fact that I was going out that summer with the Continental Singers.

International Tour

The Continental Singers is a non-denominational organization, with tour groups that traveled the world during the summer. I first saw the Continentals perform when we were vacationing in Lakeside, Ohio. I auditioned for the tour but wasn't accepted until the second audition. I traveled to Finland, Sweden, Denmark and Leningrad, Russia and all over the U.S. This gave me a great opportunity to travel and sing. I also enjoyed the other kids on tour but tired of the constant focus on religion.

Our tour director, Fred, wanted all the girls to wear gold chains when we performed, so we would look alike. My SDA upbringing had been so strict and ingrained in me that I couldn't even justify wearing the necklace. If I was going to be religious I had to follow the rules I was raised with. I couldn't see a way to be religious and not follow the SDA beliefs or to be a Christian and go to church on Sunday, wear jewelry, etc.

But by the end of that summer, I was *over* religion and all the pressures that came with it. After the tour I went back to Tennessee and found I had some crazy suite-mates. We had a blast and partied most of my sophomore year.

Rape

Early during that year I dated a guy for a while, nothing too serious. His car was broken down when we dated so hung out on campus. After we broke up I ran into him one afternoon. He wanted to take me for a ride, since I never had gotten to ride in his souped-up Monte Carlo and I loved muscle cars. So we went for a little ride and wound up at some guy's mobile trailer. I asked him what we were doing there. He introduced me to the guy and they proceeded to drink beer and talk while I sat there. I didn't like beer then so I just kind of hung out.

The next thing I know he attacked me and was hell bent on "getting some." I fought and fought and told him no, but he was drunk and stronger than I was.

I learned about date rape that day, long before the term was officially coined. I felt horrible. But mostly, I was scared to death that I could be pregnant.

Although I was traumatized by being taken against my will, once my period started, I was relieved and chalked it up to dealing with an asshole I never should have dated in the first place. I think it was the effect of the alcohol; I had never seen him act that way before. It was ugly, and I found a place to bury it deep inside. Over the years I became a master at burying feelings I didn't want to deal with, and avoiding confrontation in uncomfortable situations.

Another University!

Although I had a lot of fun that year with my suite mates I wasn't happy at that college. My parents were moving again, back to Chicago, which would be only two hours from another SDA university in Michigan. So I decided to transfer there, to be close to home. (Lots of moving, lots of schools; no stability!)

My junior year I found myself in a school where people actually studied on Saturday night! There were a lot of pre-med majors. I went through several room-mates *again* and finally connected with one I got along with quite well. We snuck off campus regularly, went drinking, dancing and partying. Both universities I attended didn't allow drinking, dancing, wearing jewelry or having TVs in dorm rooms. A lot of my behavior qualified for getting me kicked out—I just never got caught in college.

I actually made some pretty good friends at my new school. My best friend introduced me to a guy she thought I would like. He was willing to tutor me in calculus, which I was struggling with. We started dating and I was crazy about him. His family was close and they all seemed to love and accept me. We were having *so* much fun!

I worked for the graduate dean's office and again built a strong bond with the women I worked with. My boss was my mother's age. How I wished my mom could have been like her! This woman was *so* supportive of anything her children did.

I got really close with the other secretary in our office. She was a few years older than I. We hung out quite a bit and really enjoyed each other's company. There was a lot of laughter and her husband loved my "Mr. Tudball and Mrs. Wiggins" impressions from the Carol Burnett show. So I had a small support system in college and found some people who really liked me and enjoyed my company. This was new.

$$$

Funny, as miserable as my school experiences were, when I look back there was always *one* person who was there for me. One person who listened and really seemed to care about me. And it was usually a faculty member or person I worked with. The "older" friendship connection or maybe it was parental substitution?

But I had a rough year scholastically my junior year and decided to change my major from Accounting to Business Management & Organization. I had suddenly realized that I enjoyed working with people and didn't feel being a CPA was the right thing for me. This meant I would have to attend for two extra quarters and finish college after everyone else in my classes had graduated.

Well, the love of my life went on a summer study tour in Europe. While he was gone I mustered all the self discipline I could and thinned down to 110 pounds and looked awesome.

About a week before I was to go with his dad to meet him—he wrote and told me the news. He had gotten involved with another girl on the tour and wanted to be with her. To make matters worse, she went to the college I did in Tennessee. I knew who she was and had never liked her.

I felt so betrayed! How could he continue to write me letters all summer and not *tell* me? His parents were very upset with him, and told me how badly they felt for me. All that getting in shape for nothing! This was a pain that just tore my heart out. I was so crazy about him, spent the entire summer pining away for him and sculpting this great body to surprise him and it was all gone in an instant.

Living Off Campus

At the start of my senior year I had a chance to move off campus and get out of the dorm. I lived at my ex-boyfriend's grandmother's house. His parents still liked me and were okay with it. I could look out for Grandma. I jumped at the offer, although the accommodations weren't the best. I had regular battles with roaches and mice.

My bulimia got chronically worse. I felt so out of control I thought I would never see a normal day. I still didn't know it was bulimia—the disorder wasn't a well-publicized issue in 1980.

Sometimes, because I had very little money, I found it difficult to get my food fix when life dealt the blows I couldn't handle. Desperation ruled these moments. One night at 11:00, I called a girlfriend who lived on campus and drove several miles to borrow a couple of dollars so I could go and buy three king-size Snickers bars. All of which I devoured before crashing into bed.

I found a book called *Help Lord—The Devil Wants Me Fat* and proceeded to do the fast described in the book. I consumed only water for ten days and did I look great! But I had *no* energy. Unfortunately, this ended right before Christmas break, holiday season, sweets…

Over Christmas I went to a camp in northern Michigan with my family. I met a guy there who seemed pretty interested in me. This was the second relationship where I got close with the parents, and was gaga over him. He was in chiropractic school in St. Louis. His parents lived around the corner from me in Michigan.

I saw him a couple of times when he was home to visit and we talked frequently on the phone. I attended summer school so I could finish my degree by December.

Pregnant

In August I found myself ill with morning sickness. The decision to end the pregnancy was a nonissue to me because #1, I really didn't want kids and #2, I wasn't going to give up all I had worked for and have a kid that I didn't want. I drove to St. Louis where my boyfriend had a clinic lined up. I was *so* sick driving there from Michigan.

When I told my best friend about the abortion, she couldn't handle it, and stopped talking to me. I couldn't believe how she judged me; after all, it was my life, not hers. Being a newlywed she just couldn't accept what I had done. When I needed her the most, she left me, stranded—with no one to lean on or talk to. (I didn't tell anyone in my family.)

I ended up moving two more times before the school year was over. I lived for a short time in the basement of my friend from work. She had two young boys and was really struggling with the way her life was unfolding. She shared with me that if she had it to do over again she wouldn't have had them. This was a defining moment for me, I already felt no desire to have children and here was someone who was validating that feeling for me.

The last few months of college I spent counting the days until it was over, as I had done much of my life. I was always waiting until this or that happened when life would be back on track and I would be happy, and thin.

College—Weight Fluctuations

One of my heavier moments. This was the summer before we moved back to Chicago.

I was probably 125 pounds here. Ugh!

This was my junior year at college. I'm probably 112-114 or so here. Fitting back into my painter paints from high school with my Barbra Streisand Star Is Born *"do".*

Chapter 5

∾⧢∾

Bulimia and My Career

A lot of people are afraid of heights.
Not me, I'm afraid of widths.
—Steven Wright

I t was always about a career. I knew what I wanted
and with college over I was now ready to develop
into a budding executive just like my father. I was
finally out of school, done with studying and so ready
for the freedom that being on my own would bring.

When I graduated I moved to Rockville, Maryland
to be The Personnel Assistant in the Human Resources
Department of an Adventist Hospital there. I was on
my way to becoming a hospital president and doing it
on my own—not in my father's hospital.

Intro to Politics

It was awesome finally being on my own! I had a
brand new apartment and enjoyed furnishing it. Then

I found a whole new set of pressures waiting for me at my new job: corporate politics. Up to then my philosophy had always been, "If I liked you, you knew it; if I didn't, you knew it." I didn't play games, and I couldn't understand all this bullshit going on around me in the workplace. I had a great boss, who was very understanding (I *was* a handful!) and tried to coach me through. But this wasn't sitting well with me.

The main source of my problems was the accounting manager. He treated me as though I was a lowly something or other, and one day I told him (honestly) what I thought of the situation.

To my surprise, instead of backing me up, my boss told me I had to go apologize and find a way to work with him. *What?* How was I supposed to do that? And so, the beginning of many years of stress...torn between wanting to say what was on my mind and playing along (keeping quiet) for the betterment of my career—when I didn't agree with the game playing. Enter corporate politics. So to deal with it I would eat, or shop, or both!

Life in Maryland

Many days I was lethargic from the intense carb overload from bingeing. It was all I could do to get out of bed in the morning. I knew the people I worked with could see the difference in my size as I gained and lost weight (usually 5 to 10 pounds). I was embarrassed, but I couldn't stop myself. I was not above throwing away a half-eaten bag of Oreo cookies at night, only to rescue them from the trash the next day. I even had some "binge-buddies" who would go out with me and we would eat until we couldn't move. I don't think they had any idea that this was something I struggled with on a daily basis.

As time went on and the work pressure increased I tried alternatives to eating. Once I headed out for a drive to blow off steam and ended up in downtown D.C. There I got into an accident with a cab. It wasn't my fault, but I had damage on my rear bumper. So, the driving thing wasn't exactly a great idea for times when I was upset.

I also did my fair share of drinking in those years, and went to a lot of concerts. Since this was something I couldn't do at home I was making up for lost time.

ॐ ॐ ॐ

A number of guys came in and out of my life during this time. Some I was crazy about, others who were crazy about me but I wasn't really interested in them (a broken record). I was stretching my wings and finally enjoying my freedom and making my own choices. I again made several friends who were older than I was and usually hung out with them. I was having fun at last, but I couldn't seem to control my weight.

About two months after I arrived in Maryland, I found myself pregnant again—barely six months after the first time. I felt like *such* an idiot! There was no excuse for this to happen again.

The second time around was harder on me emotionally and more painful simply because I was so pissed at myself. Yet, there was no question what I would do. Actually, the hardest thing was figuring out how to get to the doctor and back home, since I couldn't drive afterwards. Since I was new in town and in a brand new job I didn't have a lot of options. A friend from college had introduced me to this guy (the father) and he was beautiful! All I had wanted was to feel some love and affection, some acceptance from him. Of course, this was the end of the very brief relationship and soon I was miserable and alone again. My bingeing continued.

Though I couldn't see it at the time, it was my lack of self-esteem that had sent me down yet another dark path—and I hadn't been strong enough to find my way out. Looking for acceptance through sex certainly wasn't the answer.

&. &. &.

There was an interesting "theme" while I was in Maryland. At different times several guys I had been involved with in college called. The guy who had broken my heart so bad while on tour in Europe called me the night before he was getting married to *her*. I

asked whatever possessed him to call me, was he calling to apologize? Was he having second thoughts? He
wasn't even sure and that just messed with my head.

I got a call from a younger guy I met in college. I
was in a singing group with his brother; he was still
in high school at the time. He wanted to try again and
I told him I just couldn't do it. I was starting a new
career, climbing up the ladder, learning all about politics—and he was black. I figured it would be way too
much drama. This tore at me because I really liked
him and I could hear how hurt he was.

Then the guy who had gotten me pregnant the first
time called and wanted to see me again. In one of my
most inspired moments I told him he would have to
come to Maryland for that to happen. He did—and I still
catered to him the whole time he was there. He was in
school and had no money. I took us to the World Series
(this was in '83) and paid for everything. He was
spoiled rotten, expected me to do everything for him.
I am fortunate that the relationship didn't work out.
I had been so smitten with him, but later found out he
had gotten his ex-girlfriend pregnant the same summer
I was. I wasn't doing a great job of picking men!

This was the beginning of me letting men treat
me bad. I couldn't see it at the time, but I let many
of them walk all over me in my quest for love and
affection. I sat and waited for the phone to ring and
felt the excruciating pain when the guys who promised to call never did. There were even a couple of

guys who stood me up and my self-esteem was so low I went out with them again.

I made the mistake of dating a guy at work who just happened to work for the big bad accounting manager. I learned the pitfalls of dating a person from work there in my first job. When I broke up with him everyone was in my face about it, and wanted us to get back together. And everyone seemed to know all about what the "issues" were. I was pissed!

My boss added undue pressure when he insisted that I start my MBA that first year out of college. He even put this stipulation in my performance evaluation! School was painful and I was just starting to enjoy life without it. I didn't get the kind of grades they told me in college I needed to work at the "best" employers. It's funny, after stressing about my GPA all through college, no one *ever* asked for it in interviews.

One of my problems had always been lack of concentration. I was a terrible procrastinator and usually stayed up half the night cramming for tests. I was *so* glad to be out of school and just starting to breathe and here this guy was, insisting that I needed to go back. Yet another scenario of someone telling me what I "had" to do without being interested in what I wanted. Yes, I felt I needed to get my MBA but wasn't ready to start yet...but I did.

My performance evaluation was an issue for another reason. I was always the model employee and exceeded people's expectations of me on the job. Now I was being dinged for a few things, including my ability to work well with others and being "moody." Moody? What was that? I had an inkling where it was coming from. When I binged I was so lethargic that I was very withdrawn the next day at work. It may have been the first little light bulb that went on telling me how much this behavior was affecting my life. And now the thing I wanted most in life, a successful career, was being affected.

&. &. &.

I continued the habit of weighing and measuring myself *every* Sunday, without fail. It was such an easy way to judge and berate myself and occasionally find a little inspiration. My weight hadn't been stable since fourteen and I was now twenty-two.

The second year in Maryland, I started hanging out with a friend from work. I occasionally stayed with her and her husband at their place. Her husband and I talked about his frustration with their relationship. They were both several years younger than I, high school sweethearts, and he was questioning if he had made a mistake. In my longing for love and acceptance the first time he kissed me I readily responded. It never evolved beyond a few kisses.

Of course, I knew it wasn't a good thing for me to be involved with a married man, but I was so desperate for someone to notice me, to tell me that I was attractive and worth having. He took great care of me and was so attentive. I never had a guy be that nice to me before; too bad he belonged to someone else.

This was a familiar place—feeling conflict about doing something I probably shouldn't. But it felt good, and I needed to feel good. Then I noticed that many of my friend's *husbands* seemed to relate really easily to me. With my unique tomboyish ways, we had an easy bond of friendship over sports—quite different than with most of my female friends.

To this day I don't think there is anything I specifically did to encourage it. I've always gotten along well with men, it just happened, there was an easy connection. This made it kind of awkward for my female friends as they had the typical wife/husband gripes.

The fun in Maryland subsided when some of my friends moved away. I was unhappy being so far from home. The countryside was beautiful and I loved being near the beach, but I barely made enough money to drive back and forth to work every week.

It was difficult to make any strong connections with people in Maryland. Contrary to the Midwest, where people moved all the time, these people had grown up locally, gone to school there and stayed there. They hung out as families and were close knit. They were friendly and would invite me over, but I always felt I was intruding when I visited, I didn't fit in. I wanted to go back to Chicago.

On top of that, working for an Adventist hospital was more than I could take. One Monday when I returned from a weekend in Chicago I heard that someone saw me "having a drink with my friends." And? I didn't profess to be an SDA any more and knew there weren't any enforceable rules at the hospital about my behavior outside of work. I had had enough of "SDA-Ville."

I tried to get a new job in Chicago from Maryland, but no one responded to the resumes I sent. So I decided to take the plunge and move back without a job. I could stay at my parent's house for a little while and spend some time with my younger siblings. I knew this could be difficult since I was just starting to stretch my wings. My brother, Donnie, was fifteen and excited that I was coming home so we could hang out. I flew my eleven-year-old sister, Keri, out to ride with me as I drove back to Chicago.

Early Career—She's Up She's Down

This is shortly after I started the new career. It was taken by the guy I dated who worked for the big bad accounting manager. I weighed 118 pounds here. But my eyes look more peaceul. The sullen intense look from childhood is gone for the moment.

This was taken right before I moved back to Chicago in February of '84. I had managed to avoid the huge binges once I decided to move, and lose some weight. I actually look pretty happy here.

Chapter Six

Men—The Serious Ones

Moving back to Chicago seemed a good decision. I'd have my run of the third floor so I had my own space even though I was living with my parents. It was difficult having to play by their rules again, but the bingeing wasn't quite as bad—because it was difficult to hide.

But I continued to find relationships that weren't good for me and my downward spiral continued. I got involved with another married man and a kid who was eighteen. Both were short-lived rendezvous.

Shortly after my return to Chicago, I went to a Weight Watchers meeting with Keri. She had been battling *her* weight since she was four or five. She had more than 20 pounds she needed to lose and she was all of twelve.

I weighed in at 118, desperate to lose 8 or 10 pounds. The women made me stand up as the meeting started.

"Isn't it cute, this young girl has come to the meeting?" she said. "Honey, we're not into anorexia here."

True, I wasn't 50 pounds overweight, but I was far from wasting away and not in good shape. *No* one understood what I was going through.

My First Serious Relationship

I met a guy at my new job, let's call him Thurston, and he asked me out (another work relationship!). I told him we had to keep it quiet because I didn't want people to know. Finally, I had met someone who was a professional, seemed to be responsible and was fun to be with.

One of the biggest issues was his mother. Thurston was the responsible one in his family. There were five other siblings, but he was the only one who ran when she called. This was increasingly irritating to me, in addition to the fact she had made it clear that I wasn't good enough for her son.

We talked about marriage. He wanted kids and, since he was raised Catholic although he never went to church, wanted *them* raised Catholic. I still didn't want kids and even though I wasn't religious any more, I knew my parents couldn't deal with this. The talks continued until I finally agreed to have children I didn't want, and raise them with a religious upbringing I didn't agree with. Once I agreed—we were engaged. This would be good!

I had an uneasy feeling about what I was doing, but I was finally engaged to be married and I had this beautiful *big*, pear-shaped diamond engagement ring that I loved. As I planned for a large wedding with eight bridesmaids, the uneasiness grew. I tried to just make it go away and tell myself it would be fine. But somehow I knew it wasn't right. And just how exactly do you hide from your parents that your offspring are Catholic? Not so subtle.

There were plenty of issues in the relationship. I was subtly forced to give up my friends and hang out with his. Everything was done *his* way. If I suggested we go out to eat, I had to pay—after all it had been my idea, not his. Thurston had big issues with the SDA beliefs in my family and often told me how "stupid" it was. I wasn't SDA, but the sheer putdown of my family was very uncomfortable.

Many things were *below* him and he had an arrogance about life that I wasn't really buying into. Our relationship was very "intellectual" and focused on helping each other climb the career ladder. My other relationships had much more heat, animal attraction and sex. I thought this was kind of odd. But hey, I wasn't alone anymore.

I took a new job as a consultant implementing payroll/personnel systems. I traveled every week to my client sites. I loved this work and enjoyed being on the road. The second year I was there I met this guy at a training class—there was an instant and very intense mutual attraction. We were both engaged to be married—interesting coincidence. I had never felt this type of excitement with my fiancé. I knew some-thing was wrong if I was *this* attracted to someone else when I was engaged to be married.

I spent five years with Thurston and almost married him. Fortunately, I woke up before it was too late. I "came to" one evening on the way home from the grocery store with Thurston. We got into a petty discussion about why I bought ingredients for margaritas.

"Are you trying to get me drunk?" he asked.

"Well, this is going to be fun—thirty years of it's your fault," I replied. I suddenly realized I was sign-ing up to live a lie and couldn't do it. I went to Den-ver for the weekend to see my family and decided to call it off. To my surprise my parents were ecstatic. When I asked why, they said they didn't like the way he controlled me—huh? Soon I realized, Mr. Intel-lectual had definitely been *very* controlling; I just hadn't seen it.

Bulimia Diagnosed

In late '83, I read an article about bulimia. It sounded like what I was dealing with, except I had never thrown up or used laxatives to "purge." Instead I was yo-yoing my way through life bingeing and dieting. In '85 I decided to find a counselor and see if I was bulimic and if he could help me. I spent eight months in counseling and was able to understand how my bulimia had come to be. There were several key contributors:

✧ A strict, religious upbringing
✧ Raised by a very controlling mother, a perfectionist
✧ Never received unconditional love, never measured up, was never enough
✧ Caught up in the model/media hype of the "Barbie" shape—which I didn't have
✧ Being labeled "28 triple A" by older boys when I was in fourth grade
✧ Being called Lardo because I didn't have a flat stomach
✧ Not encouraged to express myself or my feelings
✧ Low self-esteem

When I asked my counselor after eight months if I needed to continue counseling, since we had diagnosed the whys, he said no and agreed that I had a handle on it. But all I had was a diagnosis. I still didn't know *how* to fix my problem.

Looking back, it would have been nice to get help, while I was still in my twenties, learning to express myself and learning to identify what I was feeling, but I guess it wasn't time. I'm not sure how much growth I could have done while in a controlling relationship. I was still with Thurston at the time.

So I called off my engagement and was sure my future was with a new man I'd met. He had gotten married, but I was *sure* he was going to leave her.

The Affair

We were involved within a month of his wedding. I was okay starting out sneaking around because I *knew* it wasn't going to stay this way. I turned myself inside out to be what he wanted. So I hung in there and pined for my love. It was so exciting and I found those passionate feelings I was missing with Thurston. I was stunned to find out several months later that his wife was seven months pregnant.

I felt the strange, yet familiar, feeling of not being good enough, being lied to and feeling *so* betrayed. How could he keep this from me for seven months! I was truly devastated.

I was in the midst of making plans to move to Colorado. My parents had moved to Denver shortly after I moved back to Chicago in '84. I spent most vacations there skiing and on Christmas visits discovered it was a lot warmer in the winter than Chicago. So I bought my first house and moved.

A fresh start seemed like the best thing for me. I was finally going to have my own house with no common walls to other people. Space! Something I valued a lot. This all changed quickly.

From the Frying Pan to the Fire

When I first arrived in Denver my sister Debbi and I hung out quite a bit. She went with me to buy a new stereo system. The sales guy who waited on us, let's call him Rowdy, was friendly, kind of cute and offered to come over and set everything up for me. Rowdy came over after work and quickly had me rocking. Deb left and he asked me out.

This was the start of another volatile relationship, one that was life changing. Rowdy was *incredibly* controlling. I did everything I could to please him and followed his orders because I was actually scared of him. He was a screamer and verbally abusive. I was down and out when I met him because of the demise of my relationship with yet another married man. I figured, if he'll have me, I better go for it. But I didn't stop to ask myself, why was I so sure I needed to be *with* someone?

At the time I bought my house, I had no debt. Within one year I was in debt $20,000 because of Rowdy. He didn't like my bed, so I had to buy a king size. I had to buy new skis because mine were old—and on and on it went. He told me what I could and could not wear. He didn't like me to wear my knee brace when I skied (which protected an ACL injury) because you could see it.

Rowdy was six years younger than I and initially

seemed impressed by the fact that I traveled for a living and made better money than he did. But once we got involved, he seemed intent on changing everything about me.

Typical scenario: shortly after we started dating I stopped by his store and invited him over for dinner that night. I spent all afternoon preparing a gourmet meal and he never showed. I was so hurt. I drove by his apartment to see where he was. (Not a typical move for me! I was getting bold!) He finally came home about midnight and I went to his door to confront him. He said he didn't realize I had meant that night. He was intent on getting me in the sack, which, unfortunately, worked and I calmed down. This disregard for plans we made occurred more than once and was a big red flag, but I desperately needed to feel needed so I put up with *everything.* I baited him to go on vacations with me to use my free airline miles and I always ended up holding most of the bill. He always found a reason not to pay his full "half." This totally frustrated me. Hell, if I provided the flight, he should have covered the hotel!

After dating for six months he started to talk about moving in with me, "to help me with the mortgage payment." But, he wanted full ownership rights to do it. He continued to push and tried to convince me what a great idea this would be. He wanted to buy a hot tub and basically wanted to enjoy the finer financial life I could provide. His drums were in my basement and he was often at the house when I got home from being out of town all week.

As much as I resented a lot of the treatment I got from Rowdy and the pressure to be what and how he wanted me to be, I felt some type of fantasy about this relationship because there was the thrill of the chase.

Rowdy also had a very jealous streak and didn't deal well with the fact that I worked mostly with men. I quickly learned to keep my mouth shut about things that happened on the road because it wasn't worth the drama it created at home. It was *always* something.

He moved in a year after we started dating and proposed six months later, at Christmas. We were headed to Hawaii in January for a vacation and decided to get married there. I thought I would now be happy. For less than $700 we were married at the Westin Maui by a waterfall. There was no family. The morning we got married we were enjoying margaritas by the pool. It was low stress!

ৡ ৡ ৡ

My life was consumed with control. Because I traveled for work I never knew where I was going or what time zone I would be in. My life was more about quality time than quantity. Sunday was "time bomb day." From the minute I got up, I paced myself for everything I had to get done before I left for the airport.

But when I came home on weekends, Rowdy had many demands and complaints. The worst of which was that it wasn't his problem I had worked in a different time zone all week and was tired. I needed to be on "Denver time" when I got home. He wasn't going to be inconvenienced by my jet lag. That meant going out after I got home and often staying up past midnight to watch a movie. Since I worked on the East Coast a lot I was burning out, big time.

The bulimia escalated. I was out of town and could order room service and binge to my heart's content. I had started lifting weights after I had knee surgery in '87. When I traveled I worked out in gyms wherever I was, but never got the results I wanted because I was living with a chronic yo-yo syndrome.

I bought all the latest exercise programs by Kathy Smith and all the women's body building books I could get my hands on. I wanted to look like Rachel McLish or Cory Everson, but sadly I was way shorter than they were! At one point, out of sheer desperation, I sent an overnight FedEx letter to a female bodybuilder asking for help. She never responded.

I worked with personal trainers in gyms at several of my out-of-town locations. I really wanted to compete as a bodybuilder, but with so little control over my schedule I couldn't see it happening. And then there was the bingeing thing.

When I was on the road there were many opportunities and a lot of pressure to drink regularly.

It's a consultant thing. I went to work out and then went to join the boys for a beer.

By our first anniversary, Rowdy and I already were fighting. After two years I decided to quit traveling to try and save the marriage. This only made things worse. We had never been together seven days a week, and we just about killed each other. I couldn't breathe. I spent every day trying to figure out how I was supposed to act that day in order to please him, but the rules constantly changed. He would very clearly tell me what I was supposed to do but when I acted according to his instructions, he would tell me I had not done it correctly, whatever! I was committed to making my marriage work, but knew there was something desperately wrong. It got so bad he even felt threatened by my relationship with our dog! My life went from sad to worse. I started drinking a six pack of beer, or a bottle of wine almost every night. That way, I could numb myself to the pain and lessen his screams.

My career blossomed after I quit the road and started working in Denver. I was promoted to a manager, which caused even more jealousy and anger at home. I found a book on verbal abuse and stayed at the office to read it after work. The final verdict in this book was that *most* people who are verbally abusive end up being physically abusive. Where was I headed in this relationship?

Another huge issue for me was the two times

during our marriage Rowdy decided to "get religion." Both times he planned to drag me with him—and I wasn't having any of it. (I realized by this point I had married my mother.) Religion was one thing that I was standing firm on and wasn't budging. He also vacillated every six months on whether he wanted kids or not, I still didn't. There was too much tension in our marriage, with him trying to control everything, leaving me desperate for room to breathe.

Rowdy was out of work twice while we were together. The second time he decided to become a Realtor, but he didn't want to "pay his dues" or work hard to start his business. He made a whopping $7,000 the last year we were married. I was paying for everything, including his car payment, as he insisted that we keep up the same lifestyle. It got so bad I was charging groceries because there was no money. Frustrated? Beyond belief!

Shortly after becoming a Realtor Rowdy had a crisis and decided to go home to Texas to try and find himself—to find out what he wanted to do/be in life. That was exactly what I needed! I found room to breathe and realized that I wanted out.

He pushed me into telling him on the phone I wanted a divorce, and said he couldn't believe it. Funny thing? He was more concerned that I had already spoken with a lawyer and demanded to know who gave me the lawyer's name! The things he went off on, I swear! He drove home from Texas without stopping and expected me to be there with open arms and take him back. I was just starting to enjoy my time alone! I agreed to give him one more try, knowing full well nothing would change.

After he came back the abuse turned violent. The first time it happened I was stunned. This was the situation I vowed I would never be in after it happened to my sister, and here I sat in tears after being slammed against the wall. I had to leave for a business trip the next day and he was supposed to go with me. I left him a note on the bathroom mirror and told him he wasn't going. I couldn't risk someone from work witnessing this.

Rowdy's behavior continued. He pushed for a weekend out of town over Labor Day and wanted to do things that he thought would bring us back together. During that trip the abuse went from bad to worse. I contemplated renting a car and driving home alone—which I should have done.

There was another fight in November on my birthday. All I remember is that he suddenly *declared* that we weren't going out. I said, "I am!" and left. When I came home after a few good Italian margaritas at the Olive Garden, I found the pantry door missing. I looked everywhere and found it outside by the garage with a huge hole through the center. Funny, a bully doesn't know how to handle it when someone they have been controlling stands up to them. Finally on Christmas Eve I told him it was over, I was done.

By the time it was all said and done this was a very expensive venture for me. I had to pay him for a house I bought, and got stuck with all the debt that was incurred while he was unemployed. I was *very* upset about the financial situation caused by this brief marriage. I felt so taken! I was angry, upset at myself. I felt like he had seen me coming.

When I told people at work that I was getting divorced and had been in an abusive relationship they couldn't believe it. Not me, they said. I didn't take any shit from anyone—at work.

That was part of the issue. For years, I had been Jekyl and Hyde. At work, I was strong, effective, outgoing and successful. At home, I was a wallflower, a door mat and I did whatever I thought my current man wanted me to do or be. This had to stop! I wanted to be one person.

Weight Roller Coaster

This is shortly after moving back to
Chicago. I'm about 120 here.

My goal was to get my weight down and
look good in that bathing suit.

The effects of yo-yo dieting are showing
up as my lower body is now significantly
bigger than my upper body.

This was taken in my home in '92. I looked happy here. But actually I'm just doing a great job of masking. I was 116 here.

This is toward the end of my marriage in '95. Moving up toward that 140 pound mark for the first time. My arms are even fat!

Chapter 7

Emancipation

No one can make you feel inferior without your consent
—Eleanor Roosevelt

O nce I got through the details of divorce (90 days—that felt like forever), I was ready to create a new life for myself.

The divorce was more painful than I anticipated. I was so happy to be free; I thought it would be cake. I found out that we still have to give ourselves time to grieve the absence of someone in our life even when that person is a complete asshole. I didn't anticipate that!

As a new divorcee initially I had a blast. I told one of my friends I was going to redecorate the house with wolves, which is exactly what I did. I went to buy new furniture and told the sales clerk cheerily, "I just got divorced and I'm redecorating!" She was a bit surprised.

"I guess divorce isn't always bad," she said.

"No, this is the best thing that has ever happened to me, I got my life back."

This was my new attitude. I was grateful that I had escaped that marriage intact. Yes, I had a huge financial burden to bear, but I had just gotten into sales at my company, which increased my earnings, and I was enjoying it.

I found it sad how many kindred spirits identify with you after divorce. I had many interesting conversations about our "divorces" with people I met. I guess that just exemplified the statistics. The worst part was that most divorced men loved hearing my story since I was female and was the major breadwinner in the marriage and financially got "taken to the cleaners." They were so happy to hear the tables had been turned. I'm glad they enjoyed it. I didn't!

A few changes happened as I came out of this ugly situation. First, although I was heavier than I had ever been in my life, I started walking four miles every morning with my Samoyed, Alta. She loved the walks and we quickly got our exercise before I went to work. This was my therapy. The fresh air, the big, blue Colorado sky and penetrating sunshine were the start of my healing process.

Second, I no longer had the interest to watch soap operas. There were a couple soaps I taped on a regular basis and had followed for years. Suddenly I was over it. I don't know why, but I had no desire to watch any more. Perhaps it was a budding realization that instead of finding comfort in watching people in worse situations than mine there was hope to create a better life?

Third, I no longer had the compulsion to binge. My bulimia must be gone! (Or so I thought...) What a cool coincidence! I had a lot of weight to lose, but for the moment I wasn't concerned about it. I continued my walks with Alta, and enjoyed the fresh Colorado air and sunshine. I took the year off from lifting weights.

Jeweler Dude

I decided to get my wedding ring reset. What was the point of letting my rings sit in a jewelry box? I wanted to get on with my life and this would make it feel more permanent, over. I had a solitaire and ten baguettes from my wedding band. I wanted to design a ring that I could wear every day that didn't look like a cocktail ring.

I went to a local jewelry store to get some ideas on what I could do and I recognized the guy behind the counter. He had been at an Eagles concert I had gone to about two years before. How did I remember him from the crowd? I don't know, I just did. As we redesigned the ring, the sparks were flying. He had the most beautiful blue eyes, dark curly hair pulled back in a ponytail, and an engaging smile. I wasn't dressed for the encounter and found it interesting that in my current overweight state someone found me attractive. After seeing him a couple of times at the store, he asked me out.

I agreed to meet him for a drink and to my surprise he was in the process of getting divorced, too! He was selling his business and getting ready to finalize the divorce. Poor vulnerable sucker that I was, I fell for his story, hook, line and sinker.

I was enjoying my new role as account manager at work. This position gave me more freedom than when I was a consultant. Jeweler Dude would call and surprise me, and take me to lunch. He drove a small RV and some days he brought lunch and we would go to a park. When I answered the phone, he would say, "Hi, Beautiful."

I had never been treated like this in my life and it felt wonderful! We were having a blast. But whenever I confronted him about how long until the divorce was final, he would say, "That's the million dollar question." He was pretty obvious about his need to be discreet in seeing me.

I noticed that he drank even more than I (and I drank a lot). We often shared a bottle of wine at lunch; it was so much fun...I was so smitten, and he made me feel *so* good.

We planned a little getaway to Lake Powell. He was going to Vegas for the weekend to attend his buddy's wedding and would meet me there on Sunday (hmm?). I got there and waited for a couple of hours, no Jeweler Dude. I had a description of the boat we were going to be on and the guy who owned it. After about three hours I approached a guy who looked like he might be the one we were meeting, and it was him. I got my stuff and got on board to wait.

It was another six hours by the time Jeweler Dude showed up—eight hours late, with a story to tell. To this day I have no idea what the real story was, I was just glad he showed up! We had a blast on Lake Powell. He totally catered to me and I loved every moment of it because it was so new and different.

After we had dated for several months I invited him to attend a black tie event for work, and he said yes. I was shocked but so psyched! I bought a new dress. I was so excited to be out with him. But alas, we both drank too much, got a little too frisky and left early. I had some apologies to make when I got to work on Monday. Slightly embarrassing, but everyone was cool about it. To this day I still get teased about him licking dessert off my fingers. Hey, apparently it was great entertainment!

It was November and we were making plans to go to Hawaii in February. He told me he had to run to the Western Slope as he did once or twice a month. Before he headed out, he left me a weird voice message, something about being a terrible boyfriend, which didn't make any sense.

By New Year's Eve when he still hadn't resurfaced, I decided to drive by his house...and sure enough, his vehicle was there. Once again, I got taken. Dammit! How could he do this knowing I was vulnerable, just coming out of a divorce? I now knew the talk of his divorce was all bullshit and, from the stories he told me, realized that his marriage was one of convenience. I was just one of the side trips.

So, I got hurt again—by someone I thought I might have a future with. But he had given my self-esteem a boost. So as much as it hurt, I could see the value in it. I was irritated that I had fallen for another married man. When would I find someone who really wanted me and treated me right? It was just me and my dog Alta again, and she was great company.

Adjusting to Life Alone

I decided to go to Hawaii alone and had a blast. Following the twelve-day trip I was relaxed and rested. I was actually ready to go back to work. I didn't know a lot about sales yet, but so far I was having fun.

So I was graduating from my personal issues in baby steps. One day I confronted my boss about something she said that had made me uncomfortable. I hid my hands under the front of her desk because I was shaking so bad—but I did it, and the way I felt afterwards encouraged me to do it again. She understood where I was coming from. Wow, confronting issues and talking about them wasn't as bad as I had thought!

Around this time, somehow, I stepped into the role of the family peacemaker. I'm not quite sure how it happened, but I was always in the middle, making it right for everyone else. Me as the family peacemaker made no sense given my history with the family. But, there I was. I've always joked that I'm the youngest of the first family, the middle kid, and the oldest of the second family. So all the theories about a person's rank in the family confuse me!

I continued to throw myself into my work. Now in sales and learning something new, I worked extremely long hours. Never knowing when to stop. I found in sales you can easily create more work than you can handle if you start overzealous prospecting campaigns! I was excited about my new role, but had no idea what I was doing. The only training I'd had in sales was from the president of my company. We were not the same in our sales approach. She was much more aggressive. I considered myself assertive, but not aggressive. But I kept at it, learning from my mistakes.

During this time I dated a lot of guys but wasn't interested in a relationship with any of them. All I wanted was "servicing." I didn't care the least bit about love. I did my share of drinking and lived a bit on the dark side. There were *a lot* of men.

Hawaii '97

This was taken on vacation in Kauai.

I was a tubby 135 pounds here!

PART TWO

Chapter 8

❦

Healing Begins

You be you and I'll be me

—Lenny Kravitz

I got an audiotape series from my sister Deb that she never listened to. It was *Self-Esteem and Peak Performance* by Jack Canfield. This was before his Chicken Soup for the Soul series. The tapes changed my life. I had read *Success Through a Positive Mental Attitude* by W. Clement Stone and Napoleon Hill back in '84 but I hadn't really digested it all yet.

When I was little I loved the Disney movie, *Pollyanna*. I loved her optimism, her ability to always see the best in every situation (and her accent) and I wanted to be like her. Now I was finding a whole new perspective on being a "positive person."

Self-Esteem and Peak Performance

I began to work through the exercises and apply the suggestions in Jack Canfield's tapes right away.

The "Success Chart" exercise was eye opening. I had achieved a lot in my thirty-seven years of life, but never realized it before now.

In this exercise you are supposed to divide your life into thirds. You list everything you have accomplished, from learning to walk, learning to ride a bike, graduating from grade school, high school, college, career accomplishments—*everything* you've done. Then you make a list of several things you want to accomplish in the next five years of your life.[1]

I learned that two of every three Americans have low self-esteem. Some common signs are:

- ✧ Showing up late for work
- ✧ Eating too much
- ✧ Drinking too much
- ✧ Becoming a couch potato
- ✧ Watching too much TV

Part of the reason so many people never change is that change requires us to move out of our comfort zone. I was scared, but I was ready.

Jack talks about how the universe rewards action and how painful it is to move out of our comfort zone. He shared phrases I wrote on sticky notes and kept at work, including:

- ✧ I am loveable and capable
- ✧ "E + R = O" The events in your life, plus your reaction to them, equal the outcome

✧ It's not what other people do or say to you—**it's what you do or say to yourself after they stop talking**
✧ You are in charge of how you feel—other people don't make you feel stuff
✧ No matter what you say or do to me, I'm still a worthwhile person[2]

Another concept Jack introduces is that we pick the situations we are in, our parents, our jobs, our relationships. If we are unhappy, it is because "inside" we have a picture of something better that we need to act on.

At the time, I was working for a company that had a real "boys club." I had *never* had issues working with men before. It was always women who were problems for me, because I was always one of the boys and they accepted me. I had been beaten down so badly by the divorce and the chain of events during the marriage that I was in a very fragile state. I gained strength by repeating some of these affirmations to myself in work situations.

Another exercise Jack shared is to stand in front of a mirror and acknowledge and love every part of your body. Talk about difficult—I *hated* the way I looked! My body wasn't acceptable—far from it. These were the early steps that helped me grow.

I learned that to gain new things in life, to be able to set and achieve goals, I had to release the past. Another difficult task for me! Jack said many of us are carrying around anchors of the past, which are taking up much of our energy. This concept was more than I could fathom at the time, but I started trying to release the feelings of anger I had toward my mother due to my strict and controlled upbringing. I also tried to release feelings toward men who had treated me badly. This whole process of setting specific goals, visualizing them and achieving them really pumped me up.

So many things in this series spoke deeply to my heart and began to heal me. Jack read a poem from a book titled *Hello to Me With Love: Poems of Self-Discovery* that sent chills up my spine. I've included it here because it is so powerful...

Time Somebody Told Me

It's time somebody told me
That I'm lovely, good and real
That my beauty can make hearts stand still

It's time somebody told me
That my love is total and so complete
That my mind is quick and full of wit
That my loving is just too good to quit

It's time somebody told me
How much they want, love and need me
How much my spirit helped set them free
How my eyes shine full of the white light
How good it feels just to hold me tight.

It's time somebody told me
So I had a talk with myself, just me
Nobody else, cause it was, time somebody told me.

C. Tillery Banks, *Hello to Me With Love: Poems of Self-Discovery*, William Morrow & Co.

I learned so much about goal setting, too…what I had to do to set and reach goals. A book that came out later by Jack Canfield, *Success Principles*, includes many of these steps.

Another revelation was that over-commitment is a sign of low self-esteem. It's okay to tell someone else you are too busy to help them when you really can't. Trying to do it all is just another way of looking for approval and acceptance.

I learned about affirmations, how to create them, how to visualize and focus on creating the future I wanted. I was so inspired from the stories Jack told about how people did this. Bruce Jenner visualized himself performing *every* event in the Decathlon and winning it. He imagined vividly and did it every day—and he won!

The last tape in Jack's audio series was full of affirmations, over two hundred of them. The key was to listen repeatedly; the more you listen, the quicker the results. For a good two months I put the tape in my Jeep and listened to it on my way to work.

Goal Setting

It was late March, 1997. I had set several goals with due dates and created my affirmations. My goals included personal and financial priorities and goals such as:

✧ Attain a "buff" look
✧ Drink less
✧ Eat consistently
✧ Get comfortable with being single
✧ Get active on weekends
✧ Save $3,500 in nine months
✧ Get a new powder room sink
✧ Buy new drapes and window blinds
✧ Add sprinklers on the hill
✧ Put new tile in the foyer

On January 1, 1998, I reviewed my progress and found that I:

✧ Had been more consistent in my workouts than ever (I had lost some weight and was

back into most of my size six clothes, but I
wasn't buff yet)
✧ Was drinking less
✧ Was eating consistently
✧ Was much more comfortable with being
single (I threw two parties at my house
as a single hostess)
✧ Organized events at work for the ski
train and went to see the annual Warren
Miller film
✧ Saved $1,438—42% of my goal (*but,*
this was the first time I had ever saved
money)
✧ Had a new powder room sink
✧ Bought a new patio set instead of buying
new drapes and window blinds
✧ Added sprinklers on the hill
✧ Put in new tile in the foyer, and...
✧ Went to Napa/Sonoma with a friend
✧ Took a scuba class
✧ Started a savings account for work/auto
expenses, and...
✧ Significantly decreased the amount of stress
in my life by:
  • Getting a new job
  • Being on time
  • Eating earlier and better
  • Staying off the scale and changing my
    focus

This was cool! Based on my results for '97, even though all my goals weren't completely met, I was impressed by how easily this worked and picked a new set of goals for '98. January 1 became "goal setting day."

By '99, my sales career was okay, but I wasn't satisfied with the amount of money I was making. I set a goal to break the six-figure mark. I achieved it, with the help of the sales training I was offered through work. I immediately connected with the trainer, Donna; she became my mentor. The training was offered through Sandler Sales Institute. The first step in the process was to do a personal evaluation. This was *very* enlightening! (It was also interesting to look back a few years later and see how much I had changed.) This training did several things for me:

1. It empowered me because it taught me how to be upfront and confront people in a professional, yet assertive way…something I could not do before.
2. It increased my confidence in myself as a sales person since I now had sales training and didn't feel like I was just making it up as I went along.
3. I ended up the year at 145% of my quota. Talk about empowering!

Many of the techniques I learned from the Sandler Institute I tried first on my family. I found this to be a great way to approach problems, express my desires and pull myself out of situations I didn't want to be in. Once I practiced with them, I found it easier to apply the techniques in sales situations. I still had a long way to go, but I felt I had a roadmap to get there.

Although many things were looking up I still was very easily "beat down." I still felt inferior, I felt inadequate and I was scared. What the hell was someone with my poor self-esteem doing in sales anyway? That all changed once I exceeded my quota. I was so proud of my accomplishments and the goals I achieved. I looked for new ways to set and achieve goals beyond my financial focus. Donna called me her model student because I absorbed the sales training so quickly and used it.

I became intrigued with the power of the sub-conscious. I had definitely proven to myself there is power in what you plug into your brain—even if you don't believe it at first. Powerful stuff! I was going to completely change my life this way. I was going to be happy, I was going to attain the body I wanted, achieve exponential success in my career, have the sports car of my dreams, and more.

I felt like a new person and although I wasn't bingeing, I was enjoying the life of the "party girl." My sister Keri named my evolving party girl alter-ego Wanda (from one of my favorite movies, *A Fish Called Wanda*) because I was drinking like a fish. I think part of all this was continuing to process the divorce. Discovering who I was, acting out and enjoying my freedom. There were many times I drove when I shouldn't have and drank to excess with clients and friends. I was concerned, but having fun.

I had a very special connection in my life that grew even more important as time went on. I got a second dog, a male I called Yager. (Yes, after Jager-meister.) He and Alta were two of the best companions! They were so adaptive and put up with all of my drunken stupors. It occurred to me that my dogs were the first to *ever* provide me with true *unconditional* love.

Regardless of what time I got home, when I fed them and whether I walked them or not, they were *always* happy to see me. If I was upset, crying or sick—they were there to comfort me and just hang out until I felt better. They both had a great sense of humor, good personalities and were great playmates for each other. I know this is hard for the non-animal lovers to relate to, but these two dogs gave me stability in my life, a first.

Then I read a few books in search of some relief to get "over" bulimia for good and continue to increase my self-esteem. One book was *Body Traps*, by Dr. Judith Rodin. The picture on the front cover caught my eye. A slim girl, looking into the mirror and seeing someone significantly heavier—boy, did I identify with that! I got some insights from this book and I identified with the information Dr. Rodin shared. But it wasn't enough to help me make the quantum leap that would alleviate the brutal internal dialogue I still practiced.

Happy Hour Queen

The drama I experienced was mainly around my drinking. My work buds had named me "The Happy Hour Queen" in '97 because I was always taking clients out for happy hour. There was always a reason to go out and celebrate a project success. I would set a goal to have one drink, only to have two or three regardless of my resolve. I can't remember having as many hangovers in my twenties as I did post-divorce!

Although I didn't see it at the time, I was continuing the same vicious cycle of numbing out (with alcohol) and beating myself up the next day. I often woke lethargic and dragged myself to work, only to discover a new opportunity to drink that day. Oh well! I'd get back to losing weight the next day.

In July of '98 I a friend of mine wanted to introduce me to this guy, but do it subtly. We went to a party at his house to watch a movie on his big screen. When I got there he didn't give me the time of day so I started slamming drinks. I actually got sick and was in the bathroom throwing up before the movie started! Geez. I was thirty-nine years old. This was ridiculous!

My girlfriend got annoyed so we left and went to her house. She begged me not to drive, but I wanted to be at home so I headed back to Denver forty-five minutes away on back roads. I made it home.

When I woke the next day, I knew I had to do something. This had happened too many times to count and the fact that I had never gotten a DUI seemed reason enough for me to get myself in check. I made the decision to quit drinking until my fortieth birthday, four months away.

I achieved my goal and felt *so* much better! I lost 8 pounds without even dieting. I just stopped drinking.

I went to Northern California to celebrate my birthday. I met up with a friend from college and remember the feeling of having that first beer with him after four months. It tasted good, but I liked how I felt without it.

Alas, I fell back into the drinking routine, although not nearly as bad. The next year I decided to repeat the pattern and quit drinking for two months before my birthday. Seemed like a great ritual and time for cleansing. I felt like I had control of things now. But somehow the demons always found a way to come out.

DUI

Late in '99, I headed to Palm Desert for a week of golf. It seemed like a great idea, but it ended up a very

lonely adventure. This was the first time I encountered snobbish men who refused to golf with me in
spite of my tee-time reservation. I couldn't believe it.
The starter put me with the next threesome. These
guys were from Pennsylvania and knew several people from one of my clients in Denver. We had a blast
and even got a drink together afterwards.

The next day I went to another golf course and
they sent me out as a single. I decided to play two
balls and practice. But *everyone* was staring at me. I
played alone in Denver, what was the big deal? I felt
like a leper. When I made the turn at the ninth hole
I got a couple of beers.

Afterwards I stopped at a pub I'd seen in Palm
Desert for dinner. I had another beer, which I didn't
like, so I ordered a glass of wine with my meal. Just
as I was leaving I said something to the two guys at
the table next to me about the ball game they were
watching. They offered to buy me a drink.

One was significantly older than I, the other a
young kid. I stayed and talked for a while. The
younger kid wanted to golf with me while I was in
town...and wanted to hang out with me that night.
I felt uneasy. I headed to the bathroom, I freaked out
because I could hardly stand and didn't want to
leave with the kid. I made a run for the front door.

I "came to" driving down a dark, two-lane road.
This wasn't the way back to the hotel! I was vomiting
out the window. I had to turn around and find my

way back to town so I made a U-turn near a bridge without really slowing down. I punctured the two right tires on my rental car because I hit the curb of the bridge so fast. I thought about calling 911, but realized I left my cell phone in my room. I couldn't stay out there—I didn't even know where I was. I proceeded to drive slowly back to town on two rims and two tires.

I should point out that I am an *avid* NASCAR fan and in my altered state, figured if they can ride to the pits on rims, I could make it back to my hotel! Tomboy logic, yeah, that was it.

As I rounded the corner to town and headed back to my hotel, I saw the lights. Cops! Now what? I can't imagine the sight I created coming down the road on two rims, like nothing was wrong. They pulled me over and my traumatic nightmare began. I couldn't really protest because I had vomited on my golf shirt and all over the side of the car. They cuffed me, put me in the back of the car and took me to jail. *This* was by far the worst humiliation of my life!

At the jail, they took everything from me except my shorts and shirt. I was locked up to sleep it off until about 4 a.m. Then they gave me my stuff and called a taxi for me. I was about thirty minutes from my hotel so the cab fare was outrageous.

I crawled into bed and wondered how I would *ever* face the world again. I had finally done it. I fucked up so bad I now had a DUI. Something wasn't right though. Why had I blacked out? Those guys *must* have slipped something into my drink. I was so out of it, that's all that made sense.

My lack of self-esteem had caused me yet another serious downfall. All the stares from other golfers made me feel so lonely. I thought I was tough and could handle it, but the "what a freak!" stares got to me. I felt the need to connect with someone, anyone, and so I had gotten a little too friendly at dinner. Looking back I felt lucky I hadn't been raped or hurt in some other way. I told myself I *had* to be more cautious traveling alone.

The next day was a series of embarrassment and trauma. When I called to get the car towed, the female dispatcher laughed at me because of the condition of the car. Mortified? Just slightly. I asked them to tow the rental car to a dealer so I could buy new tires and rims. The dealer told me it had damage on the under-carriage and I couldn't just replace the tires. Great! Now I had to call my insurance company and involve them.

I looked in the yellow pages and found an attorney who was within walking distance from my hotel. But that first day I didn't leave the hotel room. The next day I met with the attorney and explained to him that the guys I was talking to *must* have slipped something in my drink. I took a blood test so we had to wait for the results. He told me for $2,000 he would defend me and I wouldn't have to come back to California for the court appearance.

From the attorney's office I went to look at the car. When I got there, the guys in the detail shop were watching and laughing while I cleaned up the sun-baked vomit from the sides and interior of the car. This was only the fourth day of my vacation. I still had three more to go. The rental car company refused to rent me another car so I had to change my return flight and leave from Palm Springs instead of LA—more cash I had to spend. I was so utterly disgusted in myself I couldn't see straight. How could I go back to my job and face people? I wasn't going to tell a soul!

It took over six months to process my case. My Blood Alcohol Content (BAC) came back at .18, almost double the legal limit in California (then). My attorney questioned me about the BAC level and thought I lied about how much I drank that night.

In the end, the car only needed new tires and rims, as I had thought. But this was an expensive venture, to say the least. My only solace was that it had happened out of state and people at home didn't need to know.

I stopped drinking again for quite a while. At Thanksgiving, I told my family I was lucky to be alive—but wouldn't tell them why.

Summary of Progress

✔ After a long chain of relationships with men who didn't respect me and treated me pathetically, I woke up and realized that I deserved better.

✔ I studied self-esteem deeply: what causes low and high self-esteem.

✔ I worked through numerous exercises in the *Self-Esteem and Peak Performance* tapes. I learned methods and techniques to improve my self-esteem and applied them immediately.

✔ I listened to and repeated affirmations daily for three months to begin to program positive thoughts into my subconscious.

✔ I took an objective inventory of the people in my life and began to seek out people who were positive influences.

✔ I made a conscious decision to avoid negative people and chronic complainers.

✔ I set some goals and saw for myself the powerful results that focusing on what you want can bring to your life.

My Kids

My kids, Yager left and Alta on the right.

Chapter 9

❧

EAS Body–for–LIFE Challenge

*Cherish your visions and your dreams
as they are the children of your soul,
the blueprints of your ultimate achievements.*
—Napoleon Hill

B y the next year, 2000, I was becoming very stressed out from the politics and the "boys club" I put up with on a daily basis at work. Then I found out that a friend of mine had co-founded her own dot-com company and I thought it might be lucrative to work for a startup. After all, this was the dot-com era. It seemed like a great opportunity. With the promise of so much money!

I lasted ten months. The politics was even worse—this time with a different twist. The software wasn't ready to sell yet and every day the direction of what industry and prospects we were *supposed* to focus on changed.

I was back into drinking too much and driving when I shouldn't. I thought I had escaped this, but peer pressure and the desire to be the "party girl" was so strong that I often faltered. I was having fun as an independent single female.

I had gone with my brother to a NASCAR race a couple of years before and wanted to go again. I planned a trip to the Daytona 500 to see my "boyfriend," Dale Earnhardt, and then on to the Grand Caymans for a few days. I was used to traveling alone now. I was fed up with work and needed a break. The vacation turned out differently than planned.

I watched the crash that killed Dale Earnhardt. When I left the track that day I hadn't known he was hurt. I had been sitting on the backstretch and we couldn't see him being pulled from his number 3 car. It was a two-hour bus ride back to my hotel. I didn't find out Dale was dead until right before we reached the hotel in Orlando. I was in shock.

I was a *huge* Dale Earnhardt fan. He was my "boyfriend" because at the time I really didn't want a full-time man. It was a convenient ploy. I just loved Dale, "the Intimidator." My basement gym was covered with pictures of Dale and other NASCAR mementos. *Eight* people called to check on me after he died—that's how bad the boyfriend thing was! I watched Dale's funeral from my hotel room and cried my eyes out.

When I got home there was yet another surprise. The first day back at work, my boss wanted to meet with me and asked our legal counsel to join us. Huh? They were letting me go. What?! They made some lame excuse about my lack of prospecting. I handed them a twenty-inch stack of my prospecting folders as I left. I had never been fired before. Oh my God, I was *so* embarrassed! How was I going to handle *this*? I called my brother and went to join him and his work crew at a bar. I drank myself silly and came home feeling only slightly relieved. Now what?

Unemployment

After seven years I was tired of selling consulting services. I really wanted to sell software. But this was around the time of the "dot-bomb" crash and no one would give me a chance. There were so many experienced software sales people on the street, jobless.

I did my research, sent e-mails, made calls, networked, everything I needed to do to find a new job. It was quickly obvious this wasn't going to happen overnight. I wanted to enjoy the time off, but I didn't feel I could take more vacation time—who knew when I would have a job again? I wish they had called me while I was in the Caymans, I would have stayed longer!

So I had a great time staying home, enjoying the dogs and taking them to an off-leash dog park at Chatfield Reservoir. I listened to my *Self-Esteem and Peak Performance* tapes and my *Sandler* tapes again. I painted the interior of the house.

Then one day I asked myself, "What would happen if I let my personal life have priority instead of always letting work run my life?"

I decided to give my workouts top priority. I had heard a lot about the *EAS Body*-for-*LIFE Challenge.* My brother had done it the year before so I called and got his advice. I bought the book, *Body*-for-*LIFE, 12 Weeks to Mental and Physical Strength* by Bill Phillips and decided to take the challenge. What better time than when you're unemployed? Twelve weeks and I would feel better about myself.

I read the book, set my goals and created affirmations spurred on by a phenomenal picture of Janet Jackson in *People* magazine. The cool thing was, much of what Bill Phillips presented in his book was dead-on the same thing I learned about goal setting and affirmations from Jack Canfield. I love it when a plan comes together! I weighed 127 when I started. Not huge, but heavy for me. I was going to be in the best shape of my life when I finished.

About three weeks after I lost my job, I met with the friend (the co-founder) who hired me. She told me the real reason I was let go...and it was completely political. I found some relief in hearing the details and learning the stupidity of the situation. It involved the male ego at its finest and I had nothing to be ashamed of—but I still needed a job!

Match.com

Another friend told me about Match.com. She said it was a fun way to meet men. This was an interesting adventure. I found several guys who looked intriguing and sent them e-mails. None of them responded! One guy wrote back three weeks later, I blew him off. Later I started getting e-mails.

It was kind of interesting to develop a rapport over e-mail and then decide whether or not to meet them. The thing it did right off was make me a better communicator. I didn't want to spend several hours with a guy who, if upon meeting, I didn't like or wasn't attracted to.

I dated several guys through Match.com, but most of them were looking to get married and that was *not* what I was after. I just wanted to have fun.

Classmates.com

Then Keri told me about Classmates.com. I logged on and recognized a few names. I scanned through several of my classes with a touch of nostalgia and then looked at the class behind me. I couldn't believe my eyes…Henry Battle was listed there! Henry was the guy I was so crazy about in high school. He was probably married with kids, but I *had* to send him an e-mail and say hello. This guy always made my heart pound.

I sent a note and waited. The next day I heard back...

"Is this Lori Hanson with the big sexy blue eyes? Of course I remember you." He wasn't married and sent a couple of pictures. Damn! He still looked fine.

I got a copy of a digital picture from my sister to send him. He was blown away by how different I looked from high school. He sent his number and told me to call sometime. A couple of weeks later we talked for quite awhile. He still sounded like the Henry I remembered. The sound of his voice had always calmed me. He was so laid back, and sexy! We continued to e-mail and talked about getting together.

The Challenge

I made great progress with my Body-*for*-LIFE Challenge. I completed the first twelve weeks in June and definitely reshaped my body. I went shopping and was ecstatic to see I had lost two pants sizes! I had never worn size four pants in my life! I spent some coin on new work clothes even though I was still unemployed...it felt *so* good. I was encouraged but still had too much body fat and really wished I had stopped drinking while I did the Challenge.

By now I had several job interviews and opportunities. One company was offering a good compensation and benefits package included a car allowance. I would be selling consulting services again but after four months of unemployment I figured I better take it.

It was time to start a second Challenge. With my second Challenge I continued to get impressive results. I always wanted to have sculpted arms and legs. Mine weren't there yet, but at least the muscle was visible. I was able to keep up with my workouts and do my job at the same time. Consistency was now entering my vocabulary. I ate five small meals a day, and didn't let anything stand in my way. I felt so good! I was getting smaller every day and starting to feel sexy. But I still had a ways to go.

I continued to date but nothing that meant anything. It was the same story, anyone I was interested in wasn't interested in me and vice versa.

Solvang

In September, I headed to California for my parents' fiftieth wedding anniversary in Solvang. Henry made plans to drive up the two hours from LA and see me. I was excited! I had all flavors of daydreams and fantasies about how it would go. I looked good and felt great about myself.

I thought the time would never come for Henry to arrive. I watched out my hotel window, then I saw it, the black Z28 drove up and when he got out I felt that same old school girl crush of emotion. He was as beautiful as ever.

The first time in twenty-five years we had seen each other! We hung out and talked, walked around Solvang, had a late lunch and I found out he was a vegetarian, too. THAT was cool! We were both raised vegetarian; he said he ate meat for seventeen years but quit and went vegan.

My brother came by briefly to say hello and then Henry (HB) decided it was time to go. I was stunned. He had only been there four hours. I walked him to the car, hugged him good-bye and realized how different our lives were. It was great to see him, but there didn't appear to be enough attraction for us to act on. That was the Saturday before 9/11/2001.

On my second EAS Challenge the inches were shifting and I was getting smaller. My weight dropped very slowly, but I wasn't too concerned about what I weighed anymore. By November 10 I had dropped 11 pounds, a total of 7 inches overall, and my body fat was just under 14%. Not bad for a forty-three year old! This was the smallest I had ever been in my adult life. But my legs and butt were a lot bigger than what I wanted. I still wasn't happy with my body— but I felt much better about how I looked.

I was determined to keep the weight off, work out consistently and continue to eat right. By February of 2002, I was down to 112 and was maintaining a stable weight. This was a first for me! There were a few times I gained a couple of pounds, totally freaked out, went back to basics and dropped the weight. The one thing I was unwilling to do was to regain the weight I had lost and lose the muscle tone I developed through this program. This plan worked!

Henry and had I continued to e-mail after we saw each other. He was out of touch for six weeks while he built his own computer. Then one day in late October I got an e-mail, something to the tune of "Hey Sexy." Whoa—his tune had changed. I liked this!

We both have birthdays in early November so we decided to get together and celebrate our birthdays at Thanksgiving.

Summary of Progress

✔ I listened to my *Self-esteem and Peak Performance* tapes again and absorbed even more the second time through.

✔ I made a conscious decision to put my workouts first and not let anything interfere. I made a commitment to my health.

✔ I started eating five to six small meals a day, with a balance of carbs and protein at each meal. I ate three servings of vegetables and one serving of fruit daily.

✔ I followed the concept of a "free day" where I could eat whatever I wanted, which alleviated any feelings of deprivation. This quickly became a free meal vs. a free day. A full day of eating "anything" left me feeling carb overloaded.

✔ I pushed myself out of my comfort zone in life. Tried new things (Match.com, Classmates.com) and stayed calm through four months of unemployment.

EAS Body-for-Life Challenge

Before EAS—127 pounds

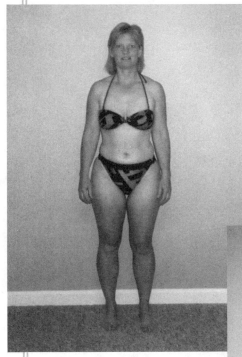

*Post EAS
Challenge #2
116 pounds*

Chapter 10

Henry

Love is composed of a single soul inhabiting two bodies
—Aristotle

The day before Thanksgiving 2001 was one of the longest days of my life. I was looking forward to seeing Henry and spending time with him. I had no idea what would happen, but it felt like we had potential.

Before he came, I had asked him what we would do if it went well.

"We'll just have to make a lot of trips between LA and Denver," he said.

On Thursday, we drove to the foothills, went by my brother's house so the kids (my nieces and nephews) could meet him. We got home around 5:00 and started to fix Thanksgiving dinner. HB is comfortable in the kitchen and a good cook. It was over Thanksgiving dinner the realization struck. We knew by the end of that first day that we were on to something.

Friday was comfortable and easy. We went to Denver's only vegetarian restaurant for lunch, saw a movie downtown, and met my sister Deb and her husband for dinner.

By Saturday night, we knew we were really going to miss each other when he left. HB asked me to come out to LA over Christmas. I had a week of vacation coming, so we made plans to spend the holidays together.

The one thing that made me nervous about my LA visit was how I was going to work out. I hadn't missed a workout since March and wasn't about to let that happen now. Henry insisted I would be okay if I didn't work out for a week. I was nervous.

Well, he was right. I didn't work out in LA, I ate more than I normally did and lost weight while I was there. Hmmm...could it have been all the sex?! Ah, the beauty of a new relationship!

We spent eight days together and knew this was meant to be. We we*re* the definition of soul mates. I had totally given up on finding a man. I was happy with my dogs and okay being alone. HB said he always knew he would find this relationship, he just didn't know when. The nice thing about connecting in our early forties was that we both knew what we wanted and what we didn't. We lay in bed and talked for hours. We really enjoyed each other's company! There was no effort; we blended, meshed, understood, felt, and knew each other at a deep level.

In my goals for '01 I had an affirmation about finding a man, and Henry fit all but one of the things I had listed. So I considered it another goal achieved.

If I hadn't spent four months earlier that year looking inside myself and making the decision to put more balance in my life Henry would never have been attracted to me. He liked the fact that I wasn't a drama queen. We were both very upfront about who we were and what we wanted—and talked at length about our dreams.

I wanted to help HB find a career, something that would bring him fulfillment. He was a talented musician who had never found the right connection to be the "rock star" and was going through life on Plan B. He had been driving school buses for nearly twenty years. I knew there was much more in store for him than that.

Henry was a calming influence on me, just like in high school. I called him my Zen Master. He tried to help me become less stressed and enjoy life. We both wanted to grow, challenge ourselves and evolve. Since our religious upbringing was the same we had an understanding of each other at a foundational level that was so nice after the SDA upbringing, which had been so *different*. We had both long since left the church-going and organized religion behind.

Henry played the music he had written and recorded for me. I was impressed. He played bass and guitar, and programmed the drums for his songs. I felt bad that nothing had ever happened with his music. He was obviously talented.

He asked me if I had ever written lyrics. I hadn't, but always thought it was a great form of self-expression. I started my first lyrics on the plane coming home from LA.

With Henry, I felt total acceptance, trust and unconditional love. I could tell him anything and I knew he felt the same. This was like nothing I had ever experienced before. Trust? This was totally new.

Creativity

When I sent Henry my first lyrics, he said he heard the music in his head the first time he read them. He recorded the music and played it for me during my next visit. I was blown away!

We recorded my vocals in the kitchen of his apartment. It was a difficult experience for both of us because my musical background was very structured. From playing in orchestra and band, I was a music reader; I couldn't play by ear. And even though I loved rock music, I had difficulty singing "rock" style because of my choral/classical vocal background.

Henry is just the opposite, a gifted musician who can hear a completed song in his head before he records it. He can read notes if he wants to, but plays mostly by ear.

The best thing about recording together was that our approach to working it out, although challenging, helped both of us to understand more about each other. No fighting, no screaming like I was used to from my ex. HB just made suggestions on how to bring our two very different approaches together. The song is called *Never Thought* and it is the first song we recorded together.

Never Thought

So rare, so true
Never thought I'd ever find
A lover like you
Years blew right by
Lonely feelings deep inside
My life was good, but my spirit had died

So hurt, too scared
Never thought I ever would
Reach out and try again
Opened my eyes
Let you in, gave us a try
My heart melted, and now I realize that

I can have it all
With you by my side
I feel so alive
With you in my life
Look what I could have missed
If I hadn't tried...

A bond so deep
Our passion is intensified
(But) this is just the start
So much to share
Life is precious, our senses thrive
My spirit's high, and my heart knows why

I can have it all
With you by my side
I feel so alive
With you in my life
Look what I would have missed
If I hadn't tried...

I want to share my life with you
I want to make your dreams come true
You've changed my life in so many ways
Our energy creates such a positive space
So glad I found you, never thought I would
Now you're here with me, and I know deep
    inside, that...

I can have it all
With you by my side
I feel so alive
With you in my life
Got it made now
With you by my side
...So alive now, with you in my life

Lyrics by Lori Hanson, © Shewolf Music

After I left LA on New Year's Day, we spent our nights on Instant Messenger (IM) and talked on the phone for hours on weekends. It was difficult being away from him because I felt so whole, so centered when we were together. We visited each other every three to four weeks. I felt such excitement when we were together and intense pain when we were apart.

In the '90s Henry had spent a lot of time working on self-discovery. He had many things to share with me. He was good about setting an idea out there and letting me come to it.

Hellerwork

One of the first things Henry told me about was Hellerwork. It is a series of sessions with a practitioner that combines deep tissue massage with body movement. He had explored Hellerwork because he had recurring pain in his face and neck. The concept behind it was interesting, with my history of bulimia and residual aches and pains from ACL repair surgery I'd had in '87.

I looked up the website. "Hellerwork is a unique and powerful combination of deep-tissue structural bodywork, movement education and dialogue. The 11-section series transforms your relationship with your body and with your experience of being alive."[1]

I found two practitioners in Colorado and after talking with both of them, knew that Anne Rojo was the one I wanted to work with. Anne told me in our first phone conversation that this work brings about changes in your life through your relationship with yourself. It will help bring forth who you are fully. It will teach you to be freer in movement, breathing, sitting and standing. And it will give you a greater sense overall of what you need. It helps free things in your mind and body. Our psyche can sometimes produce attitudes and beliefs that are stuck in our body. Sometimes these can be very emotional. I was anxious to check it out.

It was interesting and *very* different from anything I had experienced. I found I was comfortable working with Anne and was able to be open with her. I decided to do the full set of sessions. This was going to be the beginning of a whole new me.

Anne told me something I had never considered before. Our memories are stored at the cell level throughout our bodies, not just in our brain. It took a minute for me to digest this. Then I saw it made sense…with a busy, over-analytical brain it's hard to conceive of memories being stored anywhere else!

As we worked through the sessions, I found enlightenment, knowledge and relief at every turn. The first session focused on my breath and on aligning my ribcage over my pelvis. We discussed ways for me to think outside the box—about my work schedule, my approach to goals, and giving myself room to flow. An interesting and new concept—I was ready to explore.

Through my discussions with Anne, I learned that I was in a chronic state of exhaustion from the pace I kept. I also held everything in and presented a tough exterior of "me the female" to the male world. Yup, that was me! I focused on being open to what the sessions would bring me and noticed changes shortly after each session. After the first one, I had a range of motion in my neck I hadn't had in many years (in part because of two neck injuries).

In the second session, we discussed how I knew from very early on that I wasn't wanted. Mom had told me they wanted a boy so I spent my life ignoring my feminine side. Hence my tomboy persona; just trying to measure up! We discussed my need to release this feeling and accept the feminine side of myself. Anne also presented ideas to me such as: the weight in my thighs could be from me holding issues with my feminine self. Interesting! This session allowed me to be freer. I had more movement in my pelvis, sex took on a whole different sensation, and for that I thanked Anne!

The third session was about reaching out. This was the first session that resulted in a lot of physical pain. I never realized how much I was "holding" in my arms. For three or four days I could barely sleep because my arms ached so bad. I was processing and letting go.

Oftentimes the sessions made me incredibly tired as I started to release the stress and accept the new thoughts and movements. I learned exhaustion takes up a lot of space in the body, and that it takes a lot of energy to always be in control. Ah, so that's why I was so worn out.

Anne encouraged me to include some workouts that were less intense, more focused on core. The thought of giving up my current exercise schedule for a core workout was scary for me because I finally had found something that worked with my EAS regimen. I lifted weights and ran sprints three times a week without fail and was keeping my body at a level weight, which was still a new concept for me.

By the next session, which focused on control and surrender, I was really feeling insecure. I did some crazy things and wigged out on Henry. Wanda was alive and well. I was drinking like crazy and unsure why. Fortunately, he let it all slide.

Anne and I talked about finding the inner child and identifying what she needed. I had heard about all this inner child stuff and had even bought a book after my divorce, but never read it. Anne threw out the idea that my problem with alcohol was only a symptom and that I needed to stay in the moment and draw a line in the sand. I experimented and found, with this new attitude, I *could* control how many glasses of wine I had.

I have pages and pages of journals I wrote during this time, all full of resolve on how I didn't want to drink so much and trying to figure out why I did. I knew I was doing it to be numb, but still hadn't made the connection with what was really happening. A typical entry read something like this:

"I did it again! I had four glasses of wine last night. How can I be so stupid? I drove and I got home alright, but I woke up on the couch at 2 am with a full glass of wine beside me. I stopped and bought another bottle of wine on the way home again. This has to stop!

Tonight when I go to happy hour I will only have one glass. I can control this. I'm not an alkie, I know I'm not. I just need to remember to say no. But I get so caught up in the moment and I love cutting loose. I know I can win the battle though. I am strong and I can do this. I have to get control because I don't want Henry to know how bad it is!

Why? Why do I do it? Why do I set a goal to have no more than two drinks and then fall on my face and have four or five? It's like I forget. Then I realize I've had too many so I order food to try and compensate. Fuck!"

Anne and I talked a lot about me beating myself up. She asked me to think about what my life would be like if I loved myself. I sat there and tried to think what it would be like and couldn't even make a connection to it.

By my fifth session, I felt a new level of confidence. I walked more erect, felt taller and noticed something that didn't seem like it was my imagination—my breasts looked bigger. I asked Anne about it and she said this was common for women who had been holding in so much. Interesting! She said I could grow as much as a cup size, and I did! I grew from a B to a C cup. (Henry calls it my organic boob job.)

After sixth sessions, I started to notice a softer side of myself. I was using my hands when I talked. People noticed me and smiled. I had awesome sales meetings with executives and felt the flow, versus trying to direct them. This was cool! I was really starting to have fun. Anne and I discussed my need to change some of my beliefs, specifically:

- ♦ My belief that I had to be mean to be firm
- ♦ My belief that I might be an alcoholic
- ♦ My belief that I had to act a certain way or control sales meetings

I became more aware of my full body movement when walking, and started to let go of my need to control everything. I liked this!

I dreaded the next session, which was on the feminine. In a way, I had thought it was kind of cute that I kept my feminism at bay. I'm straight—it was more the tomboy thing. We discussed my hatred of having to deal with menstruation. Since I never wanted kids, it always annoyed me to have periods.

I learned, ironically, how important PMS can be if we tune in. During PMS, problems surface that we need to deal with, and if we tune in to what is going on we can gain real insights into our "stuff."

Anne told me about a book called *Women's Bodies, Women's Wisdom* by Christiane Northrup that would teach me more about this. We also talked about my being judgmental and my projections on other women—I had quite a few. I strongly resented women who tried to control their husbands or significant others. I've always felt that relationships should be partnerships and didn't like the way I saw a lot of women act. I wrote a song about it, called *What You Thinkin?*

What You Thinkin?

You let her control you
Always let her run the show
What seems to be your problem?
Why don't ya tell her where to go!

So many of you out there...
It's such a pity to watch
Always got to get "permission"
You let her call ALL the shots!

Just when did you learn
To put up with her shit?
You cower 'cos she's pretty?
Fuck that, get a grip!

You look so foolish
Can't make a move without a call
Gotta beg to leave the kitchen
She's got you crawlin' like a prodigal

A good lover won't control,
Won't try to run your life
She gives you space,
And trusts you'll be just fine
She makes you feel like a man,
And stands right there beside you
She's not out in front,
Or pushing from behind you

What you thinkin?

I've seen it too often
You exist without a spine
You think this is a good thing?
Perhaps you've lost just your mind?

Whole thing makes me crazy
Real love is not this way
Hard to watch you settle
Wastin' life from day to day!

A good lover won't control,
Won't try to run your life
She gives you space,
And trusts you'll be alright
She makes you feel like a man,
And stands right there beside you
She's not out in front,
Or pushing from behind you

What you thinkin?

How did this happen?
Don't think it was the plan?
What happened to real love?
When did it change into control?
No trust, no safety, just possession
So few seem to understand
No one can "own" the other
I say take a risk, and trust your man

> Women hear me out
> Before you get pissed at my song
> Ever think about it?
> Why you treat him so wrong?
>
> Put yourself in his shoes
> See how you like the fit
> Now, what you thinkin'?
> Do you like it, or do you feel like shit?
>
> Lyrics by Lori Hanson, © Shewolf Music

Anne and I also explored why I didn't have any real girlfriends, no girls night out, no girls shopping sprees. I told her hanging out with females just wasn't my deal. I would rather stay at home, or be out with the boys. I much preferred to golf with men than women, because they played instead of talking the whole time. So...yes, I had a few issues with my feminine side.

It wasn't until I started to write this book that I realized my last true "girlfriend" had been in college. When she quit talking to me after my abortion, I was so hurt. I must have vowed subconsciously not to get close to another female. I had a number of female acquaintances, but no one that I really hung out with or talked to with any regularity.

Through Hellerwork, I found a whole new lens to view the world. I started to feel beautiful. I started to buy sexy clothes. I bought stiletto-heeled shoes and boots, mini skirts and tops with plunging neck-lines. Having HB there as my cheerleader made it all the more fun.

A couple sessions with Anne were *very* emo-tional. In one we focused on getting in touch with my inner child. Anne asked me to put myself back in my early life, tell her what age I was and what I wanted then. I revisited the ages of twelve and sixteen. Then she asked me what I wanted from "grown up Lori" and I started to cry.

"All I wanted was to be loved and accepted. That was all I had ever wanted, to be enough," I told her.

As I read *Women's Bodies, Women's Wisdom*, I was introduced to more thought-provoking concepts. Did you know that women who have bad PMS can find relief through changing their diet? And women with fibroid tumors typically have early childhood fam-ily issues? It all fit with my newly developing belief sys-tem. I always believed many of our illnesses are caused by emotional issues, but didn't realize the extent to which we're able to store them at the cellular level.

Potatoes Not Prozac

Christiane recommended a book that sounded fascinating to me. *Potatoes Not Prozac*, by Kathleen

DesMaisons, Ph.D. This book explores how to control your cravings and lose weight by recognizing how foods affect the way you feel and learning to stabilize the level of sugar in your blood.

Kathleen talks a lot about being sensitive to sugar. She found a link to sugar sensitivity while she was working with alcoholics and compulsive eaters. She investigated her theory that they are hypersensitive to sugar. This could be predisposing some of them to alcoholism. When she spoke to her alcoholic clients she found that they ate irregular meals, a lot of white breads, pasta and cereal, and all had a great deal of sweets. She introduced an eating plan based on complex carbohydrates and minimizing sugar, and the results were encouraging. People who had never been able to achieve sobriety began getting—and staying—sober.[2]

People can develop sugar sensitivity because of their upbringing, I fit that profile. Kathleen provided several charts that indicate the way you feel if your blood sugar, serotonin or beta-endorphin levels are optimal or at low levels.

I was all over these charts. Although this book is fairly clinical, I was inhaling it. Since my bingeing included vast quantities of "white things" and sugar, this was plugging in for me. Kathleen also discussed the effect this sugar sensitivity has on your adrenals and that it can cause adrenal fatigue. Everything made sense.

Kathleen introduced a plan that includes keeping a food journal, eating three regular meals a day (I liked my five to six small meals), taking specific vitamins, reducing carbohydrates and eating protein at every meal (I already did), and reducing sugar intake (did this years ago). But *this* caught my eye:

"Beer and wine contain a high level of fructose (a simple sugar) and alcohol, which can be absorbed directly from the stomach and requires no digestion at all...The result is that drinking alcoholic beverages is going to have a nearly immediate (and devastating) effect on your blood sugar level as well as cause beta-endorphin priming."[3]

So, my problem really wasn't the alcohol. I had stopped eating sweets years before because of what happened in my twenties when I binged on sugar. I definitely had a history of sugar sensitivity. It was somewhat freeing to validate that there *were* chemical reasons for some of my behaviors. I had always suspected that was part of it since I first learned I was bulimic. From my early bingeing in my college days I felt that first taste of sugar strongly compelled me to want more and more and now I was experiencing the same effect with alcohol. My theory was "sugar begat sugar."

In spite of reading this, I didn't break my drinking habit right away. I still had processing to do and things to learn.

Move to Denver

Henry moved to Denver in September '02. I flew to LA and drove to Denver with him.

I continued to write lyrics and purchased books on lyric writing because I didn't have the best sense of meter. And, me being me, I had to get the instruction book on how to do it "right." Henry laughed and said this was supposed to be a creative outlet and something I should enjoy vs. looking for the instruction book.

I would decide to finish a song by the weekend and he would laugh, saying the lyrics would be done when they were ready. This was a whole new approach for me; I couldn't fight it. In my work as a consultant and project manager I had to meet the deadlines. In sales it's all about meeting deadlines and closing deals. The concept of letting something percolate and finish when the "creative juices" were flowing was *hard* to swallow. But I learned. I had several lyrics in the works and spent time on them when the spirit moved.

When Henry first brought up the idea of writing lyrics I told him I wasn't creative anymore. It was nice to see this side of me resurface and find that I could actually write. I was still trying to figure out how to sing "rock" style and release the choral influences. This came easy to HB.

"Sing it like Ann Wilson (from Heart) would," he would tell me.

It wasn't happening so I found a vocal coach, Jane Jenkins, who was able to help me with enunciation and delivery. After working with Jane, we recorded "Never Thought" and I was proud of it. I wrote more lyrics during '03, this one I called "Strong," about my history with men.

Strong

I used to be so cold
I used to be so tough
I spent my days thinkin'
That I had seen enough

All the stuff I learned
I was far too weak to know
If men treat you bad
It's okay to let them go

I grew up so conditioned
No one said that it was wrong
Down deep somehow I always knew
That I could do much better
If I could only find a way
To be strong

I learned my lessons well
And I put up with their shit
Stupid men I chose
Didn't help me out one bit

Much of my time was wasted
With men who must control
When all I really wanted?
Was to be exceptional

I grew up so conditioned
No one told me it was wrong
Down deep somehow I always knew
That I could do much better
If I could only find a way
To be strong

Well I finally found my nerve
And stood up to one man
Sent the last one packin'
And now I know just who I am

I found my independence
Taught myself to be strong
Now I've got a good man
And I'm right where I belong

I grew up so conditioned
Finally figured it was wrong
Down deep somehow I always knew
And now I'm so much better
Because I found a way
To be strong

Lyrics by Lori Hanson, © Shewolf Music

Colon Cleanse

In early '03, Henry and I decided to do a colon cleanse. I was familiar with the theory that all disease starts in the colon so it seemed like a great idea. A colon cleanse is used to clear your colon of any food, toxins and mucoid plaque build up. To be healthy your system needs to eliminate regularly. But over time stress and the American diet can cause a build up of toxins in your system and hardened mucoid on the intestinal walls, which can affect your elimination, your ability to absorb nutrients and be harmful to your health. A good colon cleanse will remove the toxins and return you to regular bowel movements. [4]

Henry had done a couple of colon cleanses before and loved the results. It sounded like a good idea for preventive health, and Henry said it would give me the flat stomach I longed for. We purchased the product he had used before that was "subtle" and required doing over a three-month period. I was nervous. The cleanse diet was basically fruits and vegetables the entire time to get optimum results. Since my weight had been stable for the past year I wasn't anxious to change it or lose any muscle tone.

But during the cleanse my stomach and abdomen had a strong adverse reaction. I was often so swollen I looked three months pregnant. I was *miserable* and so worried about losing my muscle tone. The bulimia tapes starting playing in my head. The old familiar internal dialogue, the vicious cycle bred by fear. I was in tears several times, so scared I would never get my body back in shape.

I also wasn't getting the same good results Henry was and fought feelings of deprivation. I felt deprived of the protein my body responded so well to and the balance I had found on my EAS eating plan. I finished the cleanse, but little did I know what had just happened.

In April '03 I was laid off with no severance pay and Henry still wasn't working. When he first moved to Denver he worked for my brother for a few weeks, but he hadn't worked for six months.

This time, I was out of work for two months. I took a job with a small software reseller I thought could help get me into software sales. It was owned by a married couple. After ninety days I knew this wasn't the place for me! I quit in early November, knowing there was no way I'd have another job before January. Money was already tight from my being unemployed earlier that year. I was intent on finding a job selling software, but the market still wasn't cooperating.

I found a job selling consulting services (again) and decided it was a job for the moment. I would figure out what I really wanted to do and move on from there. I was so burned out on this industry but I needed a paycheck. This was a new attitude for me. I've always been very loyal and passionate about my work.

When Henry first got to Denver, things were great. We were both upbeat about him finding a new career and making a fresh start. The plan was for him to attend a local mentoring program and learn to be a recording studio engineer. Their placement program turned out to be a bust and he couldn't find work as a studio engineer because the market was really limited.

When the new career didn't happen, HB struggled. He ended up with a job as a delivery driver and was *not* happy! He kept telling me it was *his* problem, and he was happy to be here with me. But he missed LA and hated living where it snowed. Plus he was making half of what he did in LA, so money was tight.

This was difficult for me, too. He was so down— it *really* pulled me down. He didn't see it at the time, but it's difficult to keep upbeat and positive when your significant other isn't happy about life.

I was fighting my own issues because I had promised myself I wouldn't be in another relationship where I had to support a man. After dealing with my ex-husband and dating a lot of guys who made a lot less than I did, I was done with that. But Henry brought so much more to the table than his financial issues caused me. Look at all the growth I had experienced from the things he shared with me! I was in a trusting and loving relationship that allowed me to blossom into a woman I never knew existed in me. It was all worth it. But—how was I going to help him?

That summer, driving down the freeway to a meeting, the lyrics for "Restless" came. I knew I personally couldn't help him, but it was killing me to sit here and watch him regret that he hadn't done more while he was in LA. This was definitely putting a strain on our relationship. All I could do was listen, love and support him.

Restless

Bumped into a man the other day
The one I never thought I'd find
We've all got things we want in life
And I've tasted, some of mine

Some people look for love
Some want success, and money
Others spend their lives in school
Or in search of self-discovery

(Well) I stayed with the man
We're as close as, two can be
There's something he's still longing for
And it's not, a family

His life has been a quest
A search for that one thing
That one that brings true happiness
A spark to give his life meaning

How do you calm, a restless soul?
When it's not yours, you have no control
He's so restless, restless
He's so restless, restless

The music he creates
Mesmerizes me
So sad to know in younger years
His dreams weren't meant to be

I want so much to help him
But there's nothin' I can do
Sometimes in life no one else can help
The answers lost inside of you

How do you calm a restless soul?
When it's not yours, you have no control
He's so restless, restless
My man's is restless, restless

Where does he start the journey
When the road is so unclear?
Can't get momentum for his dreams
'Cos daily living interferes

We'll live our life together
And enjoy the love we share
I'm confident he'll reach his dreams
Before we're silver-haired

How do you calm a restless soul?
When it's not yours, you have no control
He's so restless, restless
He's so restless, restless
Restless, restless
He's so restless, restless

Lyrics by Lori Hanson, © Shewolf Music

Summary of Progress

✔ I found a creative outlet through writing lyrics that exercised the right side of my brain and helped me begin to let go of my need to control all the outcomes (finish projects by a certain date, complete everything on the weekend "to do" list, have everything planned in advance for vacations).

✔ Through Hellerwork I learned a great deal about the physical state of my body:

- That our memories are kept at the cellular level

- How my beliefs had shaped my body (feeling I wasn't wanted because I was a girl, which resulted in my disassociating with my feminine side and operating from my masculine energy)

- I was consumed with exhaustion from the pace I kept and never letting go

- I experienced several physical shifts in my body from the sessions (got taller, boobs grew, flexibility in my neck)

- Got in touch with my inner child and learned that all I ever wanted was to be loved and accepted, to be enough

✔ I studied the theory presented in *Potatoes Not Prozac* and learned what I had done to my body with years of sugar and carbohydrate binges and found my body was now overly sensitized to sugar.

✔ I stayed on my EAS eating and workout plan and kept a stable weight for a year. A first since I started bingeing at age fourteen.

✔ I did a colon cleanse in an effort to improve my health and reveal my "six-pack" abs.

Henry and Lori

Our first Thanksgiving together '01.

Together at Last!

This is the summer of '02 after Henry moved to Denver. I continued to lose weight after EAS. I'm 112 pounds.

Chapter 11

❧

Candida and Fatigue

The price of anything is the amount
of life you exchange for it.
—Henry David Thoreau

During the six years that I traveled for work (pre-Henry), I had several ear infections. Once I had double ear infections and still had to fly. They put me on antibiotics for three straight weeks. I wound up with a *massive* yeast infection that would *not* go away. It was in my pelvic skin and was easily agitated by panty hose—and sex. At the time, I did some research and found I had a significant overgrowth of Candida.

"*Candida albicans* normally lives on the warm, inner creases and crevices of the digestive tract, vagina and skin. Healthy woman have a natural community of *Candida albicans* organisms that live in all three locations…when this system gets out of balance…Candida cells rapidly overwhelm the friendly bacteria and create potentially serious results."[1]

In my research I learned that Candida is something we all have that is kept in control by the friendly bacteria in our systems. But a number of things including antibiotics wreak havoc on our friendly bacteria and allow the Candida to grow and take over our systems. Candida thrives on sugar, carbohydrates, moldy and fermented foods. Hmm...this fit with all my binges, sugar cravings and history using antibiotics for all my ear infections.

I had fought with Candida for three years. I went to doctors, tried acupuncture, saw nutritionists. Nothing helped. After my divorce, the symptoms subsided so I thought it was finally gone.

Ear Problems

In October '03, I woke one day and my right ear was blocked. I hadn't been sick, which is what usually caused an ear infection. It had just plugged up. Many of my sales meetings were in noisy restaurants, so this was an issue!

I tried to relieve the blockage using ear candles, but that didn't help and one ear really hurt with the candling. I went to the ear, nose and throat (ENT) doctor and was told I had double ear infections, *again*. The doctor put me on antibiotics. I hated going on the antibiotics because I knew how bad it was for my system.

My ear cleared up, but then in May of '04 it

blocked up again. I didn't want to go back to the doctor, so I looked for someone who could treat me with acupuncture. I found a traditional Chinese practitioner and went to see him. He told me that I had "low liver function." Huh? I didn't get the connection between my ears and liver.

He had a thick accent and was a man of few words. He didn't answer my questions when I asked how my ears and liver function were connected. At $100 a visit I wanted more information! The herbs didn't seem to help either. When I asked him how long he thought it would take to feel some relief, he said, "You just need to do the treatments and when you feel better, you can make more money."

Whatever! I'm not *that* trusting. I saw him a couple of times but decided he didn't have the answers I needed. I felt so shut off with my ear plugged and needed something that would give me relief *pronto!*

I went back to the ENT, but this time refused to go on antibiotics. The doc was sensitive to my issues with antibiotics and prescribed steroid pills and gave me a steroid nose spray. Silly me, I thought that was a better solution than antibiotics (I've since learned steroids also increase the growth of Candida). The initial dose of pills relieved the swelling and took away the blockage, but it didn't last.

By August of '04 my ear was blocked again. This was after a full weekend of entertaining clients at the International Golf tournament and drinking *a lot*. I felt like hell. Monday morning it was all I could do to get up, I had *no* energy.

Stomach Problems

For the past year or so I also had been having adverse reactions to food after meals. Mind you, I ate *very* healthy. Being vegan, I got my carbohydrates from brown rice, millet, lentils and beans, and I ate a lot of green vegetables. I got my protein from soy and tofu. For several years my stomach would bloat after I ate pasta. After lunch with a client, I often ended up with gas (maybe it was the company?!), which was an uncomfortable way to return to the office. I kept a regular stash of Gas-X in my glove box that I used off and on for about five years. Henry said I was probably allergic to it, so I stopped eating white pasta.

The reactions I had now were far worse than from the pasta, and the feeling of chronic fatigue continued. I had no energy to do much of anything but sit in front of the tube at night, flip channels and fall asleep. It was all I could do to pick up the phone at work and make phone calls to customers (a slight problem when your paycheck depends on it!). After several months of escalating symptoms after meals I was concerned and frustrated. What the hell was going on?

Work Problems

I also was in a very uncomfortable situation at work (again) and decided it was time for me to come to terms with corporate politics. I prided myself on not being a "yes man," but these issues were making day-to-day interactions with co-workers uncomfortable and often painful. And the people with whom I was having most issues with were a direct link to my ability to earn bigger commissions.

In the past when these issues would surface at work, my pattern was to react by being rebellious and obstinate. Then I would decide it was time to try and fix it. If I approached the "problem people," which I had done many times in many jobs, they typically never believed that I really wanted to work things out. Instead, they would run to the boss and later I would hear about how intimidating I was— which was *not* my intention.

Now it was happening again and I didn't know what I was doing to cause it. Why didn't people understand me? Granted, I am an intense person and have high expectations of others as I do for myself. If they weren't going to help me then I always found some other way to get what I needed done.

In talking with my boss I got feedback about how controlling I am with other people and how I don't value their opinion—where were they getting that? It wasn't my intention! I was just doing my job, trying to provide superior customer service to my clients. This sucked and my paychecks were suffering. My low self-esteem was rearing its ugly head again. I was losing confidence in my sales abilities.

I hit the bookstore in search of books on corporate politics I saw online but couldn't find any. A small book caught my attention, though; it was about people who are too busy and how to reduce fatigue in your life. This stirred something in me and when I got home I did some research on the Internet and realized that I was dealing with Candida again. I know it doesn't sound like a connection, but somehow it was!

Candida

I found all kinds of information on the Internet that tied to what I was feeling and experiencing. There was much more information available than what I had found in the early '90s! Candida had more contributors than I realized including birth control pills, which I had taken for twelve years. I found several articles that talked about how Candida affects our immune systems, causes fatigue, irritability, memory loss—and affects our libido. I had zero interest in sex, very unlike me. I was dealing with all of these symptoms! I also learned that Candida symptoms are similar to chronic fatigue syndrome and fibromyalgia.

I found an article about chronic *Candidiasis*, titled *The Art of Getting Well*, by the Arthritis Trust of America. This article included a specific diet and recommended some tests and supplements to take. It suggested finding an *integrative therapist* to work with. I liked this approach because I did *not* want to go back to another medical doctor. But where would I find an integrative therapist? There was no such listing in the phone book.

My massage therapist referred me to someone she knew who did acupuncture. I called and she felt like a better connection than the guy I had seen earlier. In the course of the discussion, it came up that I was vegetarian. She asked why, I told her I grew up vegetarian, didn't like meat and felt that I was healthier this way.

"Well, obviously you're not!" she retorted.

I couldn't believe my ears! I had already scheduled time to see her but called the next morning to cancel the appointment. She later called to apologize for being unprofessional and referred me to her friend who just happened to be...an integrative therapist. Ah, the path that life provides for us!

Integrative Therapy

I started the diet recommended in the Candida article the day after I found it. I was only eating vegetables, berries and tofu. There wasn't much more that I could have since I didn't eat meat. It was a great crash diet. I lost 4 pounds in five days!

When I first met with my new practitioner he was a wealth of information and I felt comforted that I would be able to work through my issues. Although, once again, the time table for relief was unknown. The first step was to take a stool sample and perform a saliva test to look for Candida and check the state of my adrenals. He had several theories on what was going on with me and was sure he could help me.

When we got my test results there was a laundry list of issues. Fortunately my practitioner was great at explaining how it all tied together and I now had hope. I could painfully see it was going to take time. This was difficult because I still felt *so* miserable and lethargic.

A number of things contributed to my chronic fatigue and digestive issues:

- ✦ I had a completely reversed Cortisol Curve. At 8:00 a.m. my level was way below the norm. I didn't even come between the "normal levels" until 4:00 p.m. My highest level was at midnight! Well, that explains why I always feel like I get my second wind at work around 5:00 p.m., now doesn't it?
- ✦ I had depressed DHEA levels. (DHEA is an adrenal hormone.) My level showed I had a

minimal adrenal reserve. My adrenals were completely fatigued, burned out. This condition is usually the outcome of chronic and protracted stress exposure, and overuse of sugar, refined white flour and, you guessed it, alcohol.

✧ My insulin level was depressed. Elevated cortisol levels antagonize insulin activity at almost every level. Cortisol also increases pancreatic insulin release.

✧ My SIgA was depressed (SIgA or Secretory IgA—this is overall immune system). Mine was beat down from chronic deficits in cortisol and DHEA levels.

In addition, I had:

✧ No stomach acid (you need HCL to break down protein or fat). This is part of why *everything* I ate was causing me to bloat. Some of the worst offenders were my *healthy* diet: broccoli, Brussels sprouts and Boca Burgers.

✧ I also had a condition called "leaky gut syndrome," often associated with Candida. This contributed to my digestive problems because with leaky gut my stomach was inflamed and more porous than it should be, so proteins, bacteria, fungi, metals and

toxic substances go straight into the blood stream. Great!
✧ I had an inflamed intestinal tract.
✧ I had a bacterial imbalance in my system, which I may have carried since childhood. Not a virus...but an *imbalance* of good and bad bacteria.

Natural Supplements

So, I went in search of ways to treat the chronic Candida and found there were a lot more issues contributing to my exhaustion. My therapist wanted to address these symptoms using a long list of natural supplements.

As I started on the supplements I went through a *huge* crash, a.k.a. die-off reaction. For three weeks I had to force my feet to hit the floor and get out of bed. This was worse than it had been just a few weeks before. I had no energy, no patience and never knew how I would get through the day.

With the help of the supplements and removing all of the problem foods from my diet, I started to feel a little better and began to sleep deeply (with the help of 5HTP). One problem with sleep was Henry, who got up at 4:15 a.m. to go to work. I've always been a light sleeper and regardless of how deeply I slept with the help of supplements, this was disruptive and I often didn't get back to sleep.

Worse, my therapist told me I couldn't work out—*at all*. This freaked me out big time. I had worked with a personal trainer after the colon cleanse and had just recovered the muscle tone I had lost from that experience.

Here I was on a severely altered diet and just went through this no-workout zone with the colon cleanse, I didn't know if I could take any more. Granted, I had no *energy* to work out, but how was I supposed to deal with this? I couldn't handle gaining any weight!

My therapist also was concerned about my hormones as I was in a perimenopausal stage. He thought I might have low serotonin levels, which would add to the alcohol cravings in a woman my age. I started using GABA, which was supposed to help me sleep and reduce the desire for alcohol. It didn't reduce the alcohol cravings, but it did provide for some wildly entertaining dreams! But that's entertaining enough for another book...

Endocrinology

My integrative therapist recommended two books. This started my trek through endocrinology land. I got both books right away and began inhaling them.

✧ The first book was *The Schwarzbein Principle II*, by Diana Schwarzbein and Marilyn Brown.

✧ The second was *The Mood Cure* by Julia Ross. Christiane Northrup, author of *Women's Bodies, Women's Wisdom,* endorsed it; the dots were being connected!

My practitioner recommended *The Schwarzbein Principle II* because he was concerned that my metabolism wasn't healed from all the years of abuse from my bulimia. Post-EAS Body-*for*-LIFE Challenge I felt like I had a metabolism for the first time in my adult life because I was able to maintain my weight. I thought I was good.

He recommended *The Mood Cure* because of my answers to a four-part test that helps to determine if you are experiencing "false moods." In most cases these false moods are due to low serotonin levels, burned out adrenals, or deficiency of brain chemicals like catecholamines and endorphins. The book is a four-step program to take charge of your emotions.

These books are a must read for anyone who struggles with an eating disorder, is a compulsive overeater, an alcoholic and/or anyone who is in recovery from these issues. Both books contain a wealth of knowledge and provided so much enlightenment for me. I spent five weeks studying endocrinology and was fascinated to learn in detail things we never think about on a day-to-day basis.

Schwarzbein Principle II

But what I learned from the Schwarzbein Principle II was disheartening at best. All the years of abuse through bingeing and drinking, along with my "Type A" personality and need to exceed—to measure up—had caused my current state. But I ate so healthy and worked out six times a week. How could this be?

There are four metabolism groups described in this book. I was "Insulin-Sensitive with Burned-Out Adrenal Glands." It was described like this: "You have burned out your adrenal glands because you are someone who does too much! Your years of hard work and overachieving have brought you here. You may have burned out your adrenal glands through yo-yo dieting, excessive exercise, and use of stimulants and/or alcohol."[2] I did both, a double whammy. Diana also says, "You also need to be careful about trying to make too many changes at once because this will only make you feel worse."[3]

So, I needed to be prepared to gain weight as part of the healing process. That's just great. Just what I needed on top of all my Candida issues!

One encouraging thing was that the diet and lifestyle she recommended were very close to what I was doing. Five small meals a day with a balance of protein and carbohydrates at each. There was only one problem. I was on this very restrictive Candida diet to rid myself of Candida and fungus and couldn't follow her diet for several months. I would come back to it.

Diana recommended avoiding alcohol and suggested for my category of metabolism (Insulin-Sensitive with Burned-Out Adrenal Glands) I slowly remove it from the mix to avoid a crash. This is the one area in which I continued to struggle. I had cravings for wine on a daily basis. It started in about 4:00 p.m. at the office and continued on the drive home from work—the urge was incredibly strong and I continued to drink often. I just needed to "feel" that release the alcohol gave me. Ever since the EAS Challenge I had kept to wine, very little beer because it bloated me, and rarely drank hard liquor.

The Mood Cure

In *The Mood Cure* I found out that in my effort to be healthy by eliminating most fats and oils from my diet, I had actually made things worse! Going vegan two years before was adding to my problems. My brain wasn't getting the right amount of essential amino acids required to produce the required levels of serotonin and endorphins.

Julia describes how our brains are responsible for most of our feelings; these are transmitted through four potent and highly specialized mood molecules. "If your brain runs low on these mood transmitters

...because it's used them up coping with too much stress, or because you aren't eating the specific foods it needs—*it stops producing normal emotions on a consistent basis.*"[4] Julia likens these false moods to an out-of-tune piano.

The Mood Cure cites numerous case studies of bulimics who were helped dramatically and quickly by taking four or five different amino acid supplements. Julia describes her success rate in working with bulimic women. In a matter of weeks and months, "the women had freed themselves of their obsessions with food and most of their associated mood problems."[5] That was encouraging! There is evidence from studies that show bulimics typically have low levels of zinc.

Julia discusses the four emotion generators, called "neurotransmitters," and their function. These are "serotonin, catecholamines, GABA, and endorphins. Each of these has a distinctly different effect on your mood, depending largely on the availability of its particular amino acid fuel."[6]

As I continued to read Julia's descriptions of true and false emotional chemistry, all this was sinking in. High serotonin produces an emotional mood that is positive, confident, flexible and easy going, while low levels are displayed by negativity, obsession, irritability and sleeplessness. Catecholamines will make us energized, upbeat and alert and without them we are lethargic and in a funk. If we are high in GABA our mood is relaxed with no stress. Without it, we feel stressed and overwhelmed. Endorphins give us those wonderful cozy, comfortable feelings of pleasure and euphoria. But without the proper levels we might be crying during commercials! [7] Hey, I'm embarrassed to admit, I've been there!

The more I read, the more my issues seemed to stem in part from growing up vegetarian. Where do we get the amino acids that produce the much-needed chemical balance? From protein-rich foods that contain tryptophan! In my bulimic years I existed on a heavy carb diet and often didn't eat a solid protein serving in a day. My carbs were not protein-rich grains. I wasn't giving my brain the necessary amino acids to produce level moods. So, could my being a vegetarian my entire life have contributed to me becoming bulimic? It appears so, although that was certainly not *the* reason why.

This book also made some comments about soy protein. Julia stated that soy protein can interfere with the production of some of these much needed chemicals. Since I don't even like meat, considering having no soy protein was a tough one to digest. Now what?

By the time I finished these books I had acquired a ton of information and a better understanding of how I had arrived in my current condition. But I certainly did not have all the answers.

New Start

With the start of the New Year, I had a chat with myself about my attitude. I had really let things slip at work because of my lack of energy, motivation and lack of interest in selling consulting services. I had only hit 98% of my quota and missed another goal. I had missed my sales goals a lot since I lost my job at the start-up company as my confidence was lacking. For '05, I set some aggressive goals and decided it was time to start believing in myself again. I would apply myself to this job for as long as I was there and blow out my goals. I felt a lot better, but then being positive always does!

After three months of working with my integrative therapist, I felt some improvement in my energy, but was still experiencing a lot of sensitivity in my stomach. If I ate a salad for lunch in a restaurant my stomach would swell. I had the sense there was still something going on that we weren't addressing. Some of the supplements he gave me caused even more distress and I wasn't convinced I was headed in the right direction. It felt like a lot of trial and error. We decided to take an additional test to check my GI tract and look for parasites.

Clostridium Difficile

The result of this test told me what I knew. There *was* more. I had *Clostridium difficile* (affectionately called C-Diff). I had never even heard of this before, but found out it is one of the nastiest bacteria to kill off. It is linked to significant antibiotic use, and is normally found in young children or people with long hospital stays. The basic symptom when it is active (which mine wasn't) was chronic diarrhea.

In my senior year of high school I had these symptoms! That was the year I had multiple ear infections and was late to school several times because of terrible diarrhea. So that means I carried C-Diff since '76?

I also tested positive for *Giardian*. I didn't actively have Giardia, but it was in there. The only connection I had for this was during a trip to Mexico in '94, when Montezuma (severe diarrhea) hit me after I got home. It took two rounds of medication to fully get rid of it. Well, the symptoms went away anyway, even if the bugs remained! The more I learned the worse I felt for my poor body.

Putting the Puzzle Together

I started connecting the puzzle pieces on my own. The colon cleanse seemed to be the turning point where all this "stuff" had gotten churned up. I had not been feeling this way prior to the cleanse. My therapist said this was the perfect scenario of, "Sometimes you don't know what's there until you look for it."

He sent me to a gastroenterologist to get some medication for the C-Diff. I was confused. Why was he was sending me to a medical doctor for more antibiotics? He said they were a different kind.

After eight days on the medication I had a *lot* more energy. This was a relief, but I still didn't feel I was on the right path. I had reached a plateau in working with my integrative therapist, and I was still dealing with a lot of bloating after I ate. My ear remained blocked and I was *so* tired of not being able to hear. I hadn't worked out for five months, my weight was up, my muscle tone was gone and I was *not* happy. My gut said I needed to check on acupuncture again.

I am probably a difficult patient to deal with. I ask a lot of questions and expect answers. I don't simply "follow doctor's orders." I want to understand what is going on, why a specific treatment plan is being prescribed, what the expected results are, etc. After all, it's *my* body.

Whether you work with a medical doctor, alternative practitioner or healer, I recommend you do the same! You will save yourself a great deal of time, money and frustration! Be in tune; listen to what your body is telling you. Follow your gut and your intuition will guide you.

Through this process (except the eight days on antibiotics) I was still drinking or fighting the urge everyday. As I left work it was always on my mind, it was my little getaway. I finally got the okay to start working out. My energy was much higher, but I was having a hard time getting back into my workout routine. Work kept interfering with my workout schedule. Now it was a battle and one that kept me off-balance and frustrated.

As a result of my weight gain and loss of muscle tone I couldn't get into a few of my smaller outfits. My biggest fear had come true (in part because I focused on it, but that's another story). I was mortified and hated leaving the house the way I looked. Deep down I knew it wasn't the end of the world and that I would get it back. But I had been so happy at 112 pounds and now it was gone—I was up 6 pounds, this was a huge blow. At my size, 6 pounds is a lot!

I had written lyrics for *My Drug* the previous summer. But Henry hadn't been in music mode for quite awhile so it took forever to finish and record this song.

My Drug

Grew up in a world
Wasn't taught to feel
Came up in a world
Where ya don't show emotion
Take it all in stride
Just go with the flow
Don't express myself
Learned to keep it all inside

My drug
Takes me away
My drug
Think I'm gonna stay

Tied up in emotions
No way to let it out
Found a simple cure, one that
Takes the pain away
I can drown my feelings
Hide them deep inside
When I come to her
She makes me numb

My drug
Takes me away
My drug
Think I'm gonna stay

Tired of fighting
Easier to give in
She's always there for me
When I don't wanna feel
I've tried to break away
Need time to heal
Such a close companion
She's my best friend

My drug
Takes me away
My drug
Think I'm gonna stay

My drug
Gotta break away
My drug
Can't keep on this way....

Lyrics by Lori Hanson, © Shewolf Music

In late April '05 we recorded my vocals. Afterwards it hit me. I was still acting on my bulimia patterns! I was using alcohol in exactly the same way as when I binged on food. I couldn't believe it!

On April 29 I wrote:
I drink when I'm frustrated, upset, or have a bad day, am anxious or stressed. Sometimes

I drink when I'm happy and it's fine. I drink too much knowing that I won't sleep but I can't stop once the "numb" hits.

Then the vicious cycle starts, I do things like eat too much, eat things I wouldn't normally, Wanda comes out, I fall asleep on the couch, wake up late and stumble to bed. Then comes the magical moment, usually around 2:00 a.m., I wake up abruptly all hot and sweaty and my brain goes to work.

Why?

You're so stupid

You knew this was gonna happen and did it anyway

You fucked up AGAIN

Why don't you have more control?

Are you an alkie?

Now your stomach is going to pooch tomorrow.

Often I don't remember until the next morning that I ate half a can of almonds or walnuts or a huge bowl of popcorn.

Great, now here come the shits!

My brain starts to review the events of the day before. Things I need to do and I worry about things—

What does HB think? Did I lock the front door? Are the dogs out?

I worry about work, hitting my quota,

how unhappy I am, how tired I am of this kind of work, I try and try to coax myself back to sleep, but to no avail. I concentrate on my breath, that lasts about twenty seconds and my brain is back rampant again.

This behavior isn't helping your health! You need to get rest to get healthy. Your body is rejecting this much alcohol! It's obvious, why don't you LISTEN?

Last weekend when I drank with friends at dinner it was fine, no sweat, and I drank a lot! A different mindset must make the difference vs. the intention to get numb.

I've put on weight from not working out to help my adrenals recover. I am so embarrassed, MORTIFIED. I hate getting dressed. I wish I could hide until I am small and sexy again. I'm so scared.

I try to reassure myself that it will be okay. I kept it off for three years. I can get it back.

When I finally fall back to sleep—if I do—it's about five a.m. The alarm goes off and I'm dead. Now I've got to try and push myself through another day of fog, no energy and zero motivation.

It's so hard, I'm so mad at myself for falling prey to my emotions again. Why can't I find a different way to deal? I get so frustrated that I can't see straight. Feel like I'm in a straight jacket.

What drives me to the point of jumping out of society into my numb haven? It's so familiar—dark and warm. I'm all alone—no one can reach me here—no one can hurt me here. No one can judge me; tell me what to do, tell me to do more, to do better. Here—I am lifeless and going through the motions = nothing really matters. I don't have to perform, don't have to be perfect—don't have to measure up because I'm incapable, pretty much worthless. But I'm away, disconnected.

I honestly thought the bulimia had stopped in '96! This certainly explained my recurring issues with alcohol. I never really thought I was an alcoholic because I could stop drinking for months at a time, but I couldn't figure out why I couldn't control it. Here I was getting ready to start writing my book on how I recovered from bulimia, and I was still acting bulimic.

I wrote lyrics for *Insomniac* in early '04.

Insomniac

It's two o'clock in the mornin'
And I'm wide awake again
So many things are on my mind
I can't even pretend, to sleep

Think 'bout work
I analyze life
Feel the stress of
All that I got to do

I try so hard to relax
Can't dis-engage my brain
How can I detach?
I'm just—an insomniac!

Sometimes I feel like a dog
Who's caught out in the street
He doesn't know which way to run
Or how to escape

My brain is runnin'
100 miles an hour
It won't slow it down
Can't seem to shut it off

I try so hard to relax
Can't dis-engage my brain
How can I detach?
I'm just—an insomniac!

It's the middle of the night
In a house just down the street
A man lies wide awake
So weary he can't sleep

He works hard all day
Can't seem to concentrate
Before he goes to bed
He tries to meditate

He tries so hard to relax
Can't dis-engage his brain
How can he detach
He's just—an insomniac

It's two o'clock in the mornin'
And I'm wide awake again
I wonder why, I can't let go
Will I ever find sleep tonite?

I'm not the only one
That lies awake at night
Tossing n' turning
Waiting for the light of day

We try so hard to relax
Can't dis-engage the brain
How can we just detach?
We're just—insomniacs!

Lyrics by Lori Hanson, © Shewolf Music

Summary of Progress

✔ As I hit my mid-forties I encountered
    numerous health issues that were
    tied to my history of ear problems
    and antibiotics. I felt some of these
    issues contributed to my bulimia,
    including being vegetarian because
    I hadn't always carefully planned my
    protein intake.

✔ I found out Candida was having a
    profound effect on my sugar-sensitive
    system.

✔ My desire to become healthier and
    going from a life-long vegetarian diet
    to being vegan worsened my issues
    because I wasn't getting enough of the
    protein I needed to produce the amino
    acids my brain needed to function
    properly.

✔ My body was manifesting issues due to
    the prolonged level of stress I carried
    in life combined with my bingeing.
    (Burned out adrenals, low DHEA, low
    insulin, low SIgA, no stomach acid,

leaky gut syndrome, inflamed intestinal tract and poorly functioning metabolism.) These symptoms combined left me in a state of chronic fatigue.

✔ I begin the healing process using a combination of natural supplements combined with a diet designed to rid the body of Candida.

Chapter 12

❦

Acupuncture and Meditation

*Every human being is the author
of his own health or disease.*
—Buddha

L ife sent me on an interesting journey to find
the next phase of my healing. As life always
does, the path was shown to me.

I wanted to find a new acupuncture practitioner
but had no idea where to look. One day I drove a
completely different route home. I had no idea why.
I was in kind of a funky state and not paying attention to where I was going. As I drove down the
street, I noticed a clinic I hadn't seen before. A chiropractic clinic, with an acupuncture practice. I
drove back around the block and got the phone
number.

Shauna Sindo

Through this clinic, I found Shauna Sindo. I felt comfortable with her right away. She explained *why* my liver function and the fluid in my ear were connected. Basically the liver gets over-taxed from fighting off all the Candida. That's why my liver function was low.

Shauna was very upset about the treatment plan I had been on for the Candida because of the huge die-off reaction it can cause. Been there, done that! She said there were much better ways to treat these symptoms and agreed that I shouldn't have gone to the GI doctor to get more medication. Instead of what felt like a "trial and error" treatment plan, she knew just what to do and connected with me at a different level.

Shauna told me both my liver *and* kidney function were low. She felt dampness in my pulse and said I had both viral and fungal issues. That was frustrating to me—my last test had shown that the Candida was gone! Shauna said this was fungus in my bloodstream (remember the leaky gut?).

She sensed that fear and disappointment were my strongest emotions. She found some old subconscious family memories related to emotional control deep inside. I knew where those were coming from! The fear? I was scared about gaining weight and afraid that I would get fired for missing my quota.

Although I was comfortable with Shauna, the diagnosis felt like a setback. She let me know right up front that there was a bit of work to do and it would take some time.

How long?! I was tired of being tired, tired of spending so much money on my health (which insurance didn't cover). I just wanted to feel whole and well again.

I told Shauna I had been trying to meditate and had a hard time slowing my brain down. I wanted to eliminate the amount of stress in my life and I wanted to feel more centered. I thought meditation could help me do that. I knew I was only functioning at a two-dimensional level, but didn't have any real desire to find the "spiritual" element.

Meditation

Shauna told me about an audio technology-based form of meditation. I went to the website to check it out. The website, www.centerpointe.com, says this program will accelerate your mental, emotional and spiritual growth, and:

- ✧ Create states of deep meditation…much more quickly
- ✧ Boost intelligence and creativity
- ✧ Dramatically lower stress—raise your threshold for dealing with things
- ✧ Create new levels of self-awareness and inner peace[1]

The testimonials were from people who talked about how much more positive they were, how centered they had become and stories about the effect in their day-to-day lives.

With Holosync, you use audio CDs and listen through headphones. It is a program that has been proven to quickly help you meditate more deeply than Zen monks who have been at it for many years. And you don't have to try and quiet your mind, you can think about anything. This also tied into my fascination with the brain and the subconscious (from my discoveries in goal setting). What a wonderful discovery!

Holosync

Bill Harris founded Centerpointe Research after doing a great deal of research on this method of meditation. I'm not typically interested in scientific research, but this was different. I'll include just enough to help you get a sense of how powerful this tool is.

Using Holosync is like exercise for your brain. Bill compares it to a runner who starts out with one mile a day and has to work up to three or four miles. It's the same thing. You start out at the beginning level and work your way up over a period of months. The process involves moving your brain through the four categories of brain wave patterns (beta, alpha, theta and delta) with the audio CD.

"As we slow the brain waves from beta to alpha to theta to delta using Holosync, there is a corresponding increase in balance between the two hemispheres of the brain. This more balanced brain state is called brain synchrony, or brain synchronization."[2]

As our brain waves slow and our brain balances, we tap into what scientists call "whole-brain thinking, or whole-brain functioning." This means we are using both sides of the brain to think vs. just using one side, which is typical function. When we think in stereo we gain a new perspective because this is associated with increased creativity, insight, learning ability, memory and problem-solving abilities.[3]

Bill explains that as human beings we are programmed before birth and through adult life in a number of ways. We are programmed by everyone we come in contact with—teachers, parents, siblings, advertising, movies, and more. By the time we start school we are nothing more than automatic response mechanisms and we react to things unconsciously as our brains guide us toward pleasure and away from pain based on past experiences.

In many aspects of life this is a good thing, but we can learn to link pleasure and pain to situations that limit our ability to be happy. Traumatic experiences such as dysfunctional family situations, e.g., alcoholic parents, parents who aren't there, physical and sexual abuse can contribute to these "poor associations." These and many other early childhood situations can leave us with brain associations that make it difficult or impossible to achieve, trust, have good relationships or express our feelings.

In addition, we can become programmed with toxic shame and guilt, phobias, lack of ambition, difficulty in knowing or asking for what we want, an insatiable need for approval, fear of intimacy, etc. These associations leave us with reactions and behaviors that are very unhealthy.[4]

Balancing your brain with Holosync meditation will result in a life that includes more happiness, inner peace and success...

Okay, I was game!

The interesting thing about Holosync is that it "pushes" your brain. It will bring up your "stuff" and you will deal with it and get through it. For me this meant all the issues around not measuring up, problems with the other strong personalities at work, always taking the attitude that I had screwed up and wondering if I was in trouble.

I was convinced that by using Holosync I could create a new reality, rid myself of poor belief systems and move things out of my way that were keeping me from the success I so strongly desired.

Holosync will also increase your levels of DHEA and serotonin. I could stop taking the supplements and get this naturally, which was what I wanted to do anyway. Another added benefit! Check out Holosync at www.centerpointe.com.

Thresholds of the Mind

I read *Thresholds of the Mind: Your Personal Road-map to Success, Happiness, and Contentment* by Bill Harris. It gave me a detailed understanding about what the Holosync process can do for you. Another must-read for anyone with eating disorders, or compulsive or addictive habits!

I learned that *any* form of discomfort = resistance. "It's when you stop trying to control resistance that it goes away."[5] Bill talks a lot about being "the wit-ness," which is simply watching yourself, with curiosity—like a scientist with no agenda—when you are resisting (when you are in one of your be-haviors). It's kind of like being a fly on the wall, or being an observer in a situation. I have done this a lot in sales meetings so I don't get emotionally in-volved in the sale.

As "the witness," you watch your internal dia-logue, feelings, reactions—everything. *But*, you don't try to control it—you let everything be okay. This part was painful for me. I had so much trouble stay-ing out of the analytical and trying to figure out why I was still bingeing. Why I was still drinking after I had a thorough understanding why these things were happening. Yes, these were well ingrained habits, practiced for over thirty-three years but...

As I continued to work with Shauna she encour-aged me to let go, to quit beating up on myself and let everything be okay. I didn't quite know how to do that at first, but I was ready to make a change. I was so tired of living the way I did. We worked on my ear and attacked the fungus in my bloodstream with more natural supplements.

The hardest part of this treatment plan was that Shauna wanted me to go back on a Candida diet. It was so restrictive and this time I was really struggling to stay on it because I had just lived this way for six months. When I had decided to do the Candida diet in October the year before, it was *my* decision so this hadn't been an issue (still rebellious!).

I needed room to breathe. Being vegan is hard enough, but on this diet, if I was at lunch with a client all I could have was salad with olive oil on it. Then my stomach would swell up because of the preservatives on the salad! I did the best I could at the time, and...continued to drink.

About the time I found Shauna, Henry found out about someone who did energy healing. He thought she might be able to help me with the fluid in my ears. I called as soon as I got her number.

Summary of Progress

✔ Through acupuncture I was able to gain a deeper understanding of issues my body was having (low kidney and liver function, fungus in my bloodstream) and make incremental improvements in my energy.

✔ I searched for and found a method of meditation that worked for someone overly analytical like me who has a terrible time turning my brain off.

✔ Through *Thresholds of the Mind* I learned even more about the sub-conscious and the filters each of us creates to view the world based on our upbringing.

✔ I learned that any form of discomfort is our own personal resistance.

✔ I was introduced to the concept of "let everything be okay" and being the witness to study our own behaviors.

Chapter 13

❦

The Flow of Energy

Only I can change my life. No one can do it for me.
—Carol Burnett

Introduction to Energy Healing

From the first day I met Tina Meyer, I knew I had found a strong connection to my healing. Although this was incredibly different from anything I had experienced before, I was open. Tina told me many times people with ear problems frequently have associations from a young age of things we don't want to hear, things we want to block out (like fights between parents or a controlling parent). Tina told me I wasn't "grounded" and wasn't even connected to my pelvis or legs. Interesting. Recently my massage therapist asked if I ever inhabited my legs. I asked what she meant.

"There is so much energy around your head, do you ever slow down? Your legs have no energy flow," she said.

Tina also said I had a very strong will. She told

me that our will is located in our back and that our emotions are in the front. I was overcompensating by using my will for everything and avoiding my emotions. Like that was news!

Tina offered to help in removing the blocked energy and said where I was on the edge, things would happen quickly after the blocked energy was moved. She found a lot of stored up old energy in my second chakra, the one linked to self-esteem. The body has spinning energy centers, which look like spinning wheels that are called chakras. Chakras are energy nodes in our bodies.

I had heard people talk about energy healing before, but always thought it was kind of "out there." Energy work is a type of healing that is a hands-on technique. It balances, clears and charges your energy field. It removes energy blocks that lead to dis-ease, enhancing your body's natural healing potential.

I went to Tina primarily to do a manual lymph drainage and some cranial sacral work to help my ear and found there was a lot more she could do for me. The blocked ear quickly moved to the background as she started to work on my energy flow (or lack thereof!).

What the Bleep Do We Know!?

When I got home, the movie *What the Bleep Do We Know!?* (*What the Bleep*) arrived from Netflix. I had heard a lot about the movie and HB and I decided to watch it that night. Talk about a turning point in life! It tied into my questions about the new path I was exploring and made me more comfortable with the energy work. Since I grew up with Christian beliefs some of this stuff seemed kind of weird—even though I no longer considered myself a Christian.

The movie blurs the lines between science and religion and presented new theories about our bodies and non-physical beings. More importantly, the portrayal of Amanda (by Marlee Matlin) had a huge impact on me. Watching how poorly Amanda treated herself out of hatred, seeing the effect negativity had on water molecules—whoa! When the guy in the subway said to her, "Makes you wonder, doesn't it? If thoughts can do that to water, imagine what our thoughts can do to us," I knew I had to stop beating up on myself and was ready to let go of the negativity.

This movie had a *profound* impact on my thick-headed, bulimic-behaving brain. Seeing the visual of Amanda made me sad for all of the terrible ways I had treated myself, for all of the hatred I'd had for my body and not accepting myself. I felt horrible.

I love these phrases from the movie:

"We can only see what *we* believe is possible."

"Thought or intent is driving force."

These certainly tied into my goal-setting and understanding about the power of the subconscious!

The other thing from the movie that I absorbed

right away was Dr. Dispenza's quote, "I wake up in the morning and consciously create my day...the way *I* want it to happen." I incorporated this into my daily routine.

The concept that our cells reproduce with either the positive or negative influence we concentrate on really got me. *Our mind literally creates our body.* Wow—was I missing the boat! More importantly, how could I take this, *apply* it, and grow from it?

A couple of days later, I did my own version of forgiveness like Amanda did in the movie. I didn't even feel foolish doing it. I wrote "love" and drew hearts all over my body and really tried to get in a place of forgiveness with myself.

Ask and It Is Given

Shortly after I watched *What the Bleep*, I heard about *Ask and It Is Given: Learning to Manifest Your Desires* by Esther and Jerry Hicks. This book has a wealth of great ideas on how to simply *vibrate* for what you want in life. That means to be in the vibration (frequency) of what you want. We all vibrate on a certain frequency and we can actually raise our vibration with the right focus. To me this meant increasing my level of positive thinking. *And* it tied back to things I had seen in *What the Bleep*.

What was described in this book totally connected with what I was learning from Bill Harris and the Holosync meditation. It's all about learning not to be resistant. Easier said than done! I would really get it and have a great week. The next week I would be all wrapped up in issues from work, lack of money, and the fact I was still drinking and not losing weight.

"Just try to be the witness and let everything be okay," Shauna kept saying. I was trying to figure that out.

Over time it got easier. With the help of Holosync and reading the *Ask* book. I started to make some monumental leaps in my life and psyche. The *Ask* book has twenty-two processes in the back to help apply the principles. The hardest thing for someone like me is we can't *make* these things happen. We need to just put them out there, let go of resistance (that inner safety net and ego that is hanging on for dear life) and allow what we want to come to us. I was still trying to connect this with my goal setting and got a bit confused for a while on what I needed to do.

The *Ask* book talks about simply putting the *vibration* out there for what you desire. It sounds so easy: "The reason you have not already gotten what you desire is because you are holding yourself in a vibrational holding pattern that does not match the vibration of your desire.[1] Okay, but just exactly how did I make that happen? "The only thing you need to do is gently and gradually, piece by piece, release your resistant thoughts, which are the only disallowing factors involved."[2] Sounded easy.

There is so much discussion in this book about our focus and the law of attraction, what we focus on is what we will get—good or bad. I first read about the law of attraction many years before in one of Napoleon Hill's books. It sounded simple, but it took me a long time to digest because I was always "trying so hard" to make everything happen.

It's difficult for me to think about just putting the intention of what I want out there—and being in a state of *allowing* it to come to me vs. actively making it happen. I'm the goal-setting girl! There is a fundamental principle found in many of the books I've read that says you can tell what you are focusing on by looking at the results in your life. Touché!

I started using some of the processes that were in the book. They are based on the level of emotional state we are in to relieve resistance and vibrate for what we want. I used The Rampage of Appreciation, The Magical Creation Box, The Prosperity Game, Scripting and the Place Mat processes. I especially liked Scripting because this involved writing a script for what you wanted to happen; I could do that!

The Rampage of Appreciation is based on your ability to appreciate something fully, regardless of where you are. If you can stop and thoroughly appreciate the site helps to lessen your negative vibration, which I certainly needed to do.[3]

I started to notice flowers and plants when I was sitting at a stop light and enjoyed their every detail. Looking for the beauty in everything puts a different perspective on the day. Since a lot of what I needed to do was to let go, I read and re-read this book and "tried hard" to apply these processes in my life!

Energy Sessions

The energy sessions I did with Tina were a combination of talking and light hands-on healing to shift my energy. It was intriguing to me how she could sense what needed to happen by listening to what I said, reading my body language and confirming it just by touching my feet! The reward was the rush of energy that flowed through my body those first few times. A sensation I wasn't used to! I had lived in my head for so many years I didn't even know *how* to get in touch with my arms or legs.

I loved the days I went to see Tina and enjoyed the growth—and the process. This was far better than the counseling I did twenty years ago. And Tina was willing to help me learn *how* to express my emotions.

I quickly opened up and as I did my beliefs shifted. I learned so much about the non-physical beings we are. Things that I never really spent time thinking about and used to shy away from were now helping me to create a whole new experience in the world and a whole new Lori.

But shortly after starting to work with Tina, I found myself bingeing again. Talk about freaking out! I had already put on a few pounds, enough already! I recently made the connection between the alcohol consumption and bulimia patterns and now here I sat, eating a whole DiGiorno pizza with a pint of ice cream in one sitting, huh?

A couple of weeks later I learned that part of the healing process of working through the old energy and releasing it was peeling back the layers (like an onion) and as part of this process I would experience some of these behaviors again in order to rid myself of them. NO! I was embarrassed enough about getting dressed. If I gained more weight I would be back looking for my mu-mus!

The first month was an interesting series of new discoveries and living through ugly old patterns. About three weeks after my first visit, I had the single most amazing day of my life. In my journal, I wrote:

"I enjoyed the weather, drove the Rocket (my sports car) to the Springs, ignored the traffic, felt the music and enjoyed it. I had this overall feeling of happiness, calm and being centered. It felt incredible to feel!

"Then on to my massage. I felt tingling all down my legs. I stayed quiet instead of talking the whole time. I tuned in to each part of my body and felt it release. A whole new station to tune in to. Before today I had only excitement or frustration."

I started to notice subtle changes in my life. Small things at work in how I related to people, being more comfortable in sales meetings, and getting a little better at dealing with politics.

I went to Santa Barbara for a week of vacation and started to write this book. It was such a release for me. I was able to enjoy every minute of my time. I ate at expensive restaurants and had dessert almost every night and was okay with it. I didn't beat myself up.

I bought a cheap silver mood necklace. To my surprise, for the first time in my life I was actually able to see something other than black and green (two most stressed colors) in the necklace. I saw it go all the way to purple, the most relaxed color, unconditional love.

When I got home, I wore my mood necklace to work a few times and was tickled to see that even driving to work in heavy traffic I could keep it purple. For me—being in this kind of a relaxed state was a huge shift.

By July after two months of energy treatments, however, I was really struggling with alcohol, night sweats and why I couldn't change the behavior. I was afraid that I was using the knowledge of reliving old behaviors as a crutch.

I started to spend money I didn't have. This was something I had done in the early days after college on those few occasions I didn't binge. I quickly saw this was yet another old pattern resurfacing.

Tina continued to work on my second chakra and did a spinal cleanse. We scheduled time to do a lymph drainage two days in a row, to increase the intensity of the healing. My ear was still blocked and I wanted relief! While working on my ear Tina felt drawn to check the energy in my mouth. Tina barely touched my teeth.

"You have the most intense energy in your mouth of anyone I've worked on," she said.

I told her the week before I was writing about my abortions in my book and wasn't sure if I would leave the details in or not. She said she felt the old energy from the fetuses.

All of a sudden I was reliving the whole scenario of the second abortion. I tried to forgive myself while I was reliving the experience, but I couldn't. Tina told me to let go of the old energy and forgive myself from the present and suddenly I felt a huge wave of forgiveness wash over me. What a huge release! I realized that I had completely blocked the experience because I never wanted kids.

So I acknowledged the unborn fetuses and, twenty-four years later, let them go! I cried uncontrollably and *felt* their energy as it left me. I felt so open and free. Tina told me my entire energy had shifted. I had a whole new energy body.

I was ecstatic. I had a high like I'd never felt, a freedom I'd never experienced, a peace I'd never known. As I was leaving Tina's office, it came to me—just that inner knowing—they were both boys.

Six months ago this scenario would have *totally* freaked me out, but I was comfortable with the events of the day. Now I had a *new* best day of my life! I felt like all my abdominal issues were gone. I felt reconnected sexually. I found another piece of the puzzle. This felt like the core of all the abdominal problems and lack of libido.

Suddenly I felt connected to Henry. I could relate. I wanted to see him, touch him and talk to him.

I even wanted to share this energy flow and healing with my "angry" young nephew and my younger sister. This is what I call growth! I had a proposal due the next day, but I went to my favorite neighborhood bar and sat on the deck. I had a little memorial service for the boys and set their spirits free. I had held them long enough. I couldn't believe how different I felt!

That night I woke up, not at the usual 2 a.m., but at 12:15 a.m., dripping in sweat—like I'd just broken a fever. I couldn't sleep and as I tossed and turned Henry woke. We revisited the sex "thang." There was more feeling, new sensitivity and intimacy. I wound up crying in convulsions. It was another huge release.

Another puzzle piece fit. All those years searching everywhere for someone to "have me, love me or do me." I never really got anything from it because I was closed off physically, in part because I felt guilty about getting pregnant twice. I was "bad" and therefore had just shut down that part of my body.

ۻ ۻ ۻ

Henry left Denver to go to luthier school in Phoenix for five and a half months. What awaited me after he left was certainly unexpected.

I found myself drinking almost every night. Eating tortilla chips, ice cream, pizza, and *what*?

My next visit with Tina was another interesting one. We started to work on my intention. We worked on the issues associated with my unhealthy behaviors. Tina told me this was going to be a journey. There were so many things she saw attached to my bulimia, it was going to take some time to work through them all.

Working on the energy of my intention Tina was able to feed me information about the "why" and I was able to identify with it. I knew exactly where it came from and gained a deeper level of understanding for myself and why some things were the way they were.

Over the years I had dug a grave for myself. Growing up I was in many situations where I felt I would rather die than deal with it. There were a lot of sentiments of "I'm not worthy, I don't measure up." This was tied to my heart. I had a big strong heart, but it was unfed because I always did generous things for everyone else, but didn't love myself. My heart knew this was abuse that I didn't deserve. My heart had kept me alive.

I could instantly relate to circumstances where this occurred in my early years. I remember that feeling of not wanting to be in a situation. Not being able to deal was in essence the escape my bingeing and drinking provided me, the ability to numb out and leave.

I was drinking a lot so Tina and I made the decision to slow down the work we were doing. It seemed like I was in a healing crisis. Everything was in chaos, I was "too much in my head" again and totally frustrated. Tina felt I was drinking to numb out vs. dealing with the processing I needed to do.

As I slowed down the frequency of sessions things began to make sense. I got new insights into how to deal with people at work. I was *thinking*, not just reacting.

I wanted to learn how to be more conscious and live life as a conscious being vs. numbing out. Tina found energy from dealing with my family when I was growing up. I often went out of body vs. dealing with my mom, dad and siblings. I could *completely* relate to that and had plenty of examples when I was being lectured to by my mother, or sitting through some family worship where I just plain shut down, left the building. Yup—that made sense!

Energy from my second chakra (self-esteem)

showed that when my body was developing I couldn't deal with my beauty or my body growing and evolving because of the boys that made fun of me. So I shut down.

What's *really* interesting about this one is my breasts grew again with the energy healing. As I became more open and let go of all the old energy, I was finally becoming the physical person I was supposed to be.

That blows me away! That we can *physically* alter our development based on circumstances and beliefs growing up. Once again, more pieces to the puzzle. I left my session prepared to be more conscious. It didn't happen overnight and I got frustrated. But I could see it coming, bit by bit.

A Connection to Feminine

One day I realized something interesting. All of the people I was working with on my healing (except the integrative therapist) were women, and I was bonding with the feminine interactions in my life. From Anne, who did my Hellerwork, to my massage therapist, I was finally connecting with women and enjoying their company. I even planned a dinner one night to introduce all "my girls" to each other.

I had another female kindred spirit from the corporate world who was so supportive and encouraging me at every turn. Although Victoria and I didn't get to see each other often, when we spent time together it was always so uplifting. I knew she genuinely cared about me, no hidden agendas, and I could talk openly with her about the path I was on and what I was doing. We were on similar exploratory paths looking for enlightenment, so we were able to share a great deal with each other.

Finding a Spiritual Connection

Through the combination of the energy healing and Holosync meditation, I started to connect with all three dimensions. I spent so many years shut down to anything spiritual, because spiritual to me meant religion, and I wanted nothing to do with religion.

Henry and I went to a day-long yoga and meditation retreat at Shoshoni, north of Boulder just before he left for school. It was a new experience, very peaceful and welcome. I started to relish the thought of spending a quiet weekend at home, with no agenda except to nourish and spiritually feed myself vs. hurrying through the list of errands.

Connecting My Head and Body

The next session with Tina brought the day I had been waiting for since my first session. Several times I thought I was ready, but Tina always said, "No, not yet."

That morning when I was working out, I knew. I was finally ready to have my head reconnected with my body (energetically—no comments from the peanut gallery!) and let my energy flow through my whole body. Tina told me she had to get my head slowed down before she could do this or I would experience a lot of frustration. It was time!

I didn't know quite what to expect. The first thing I noticed was my breath, and the movement of my abdomen. Something that was always difficult for me to do when I tried to meditate. The whole "be with your breath" thing was beyond me because my mind was so busy. I also felt some energy shift in my legs, but not a lot.

The next morning, when I ran my sprints I had a new sensation. Feeling in my feet, my butt, my legs, *feeling* the movement—and it felt good! I wondered if this is a gift athletes have, are they more in touch with their bodies?

I started thinking about what effect this session would have on my sex life! On my next visit to see Henry in Phoenix I was pleased to find out my suspicions were correct. The flow of whole body energy had indeed improved my sexual experience.

Letting Go of the Behavior Pattern

I felt like I'd made so much progress, but I was frustrated because I made great strides one week, then I would have to meet clients for happy hour and would have a drink I didn't want, followed by another, and then fell to the "sugar train." There were a couple of scary incidents where I actually blacked out from the wine and sugar intake once I got home.

I spent some time thinking about why the behavior continued. There were a *lot* of attachments to poor beliefs. But I had now reached a point in life where this behavior no longer served me. It was simply time to let go.

I set my intention to live consciously. I believe the blackouts happened because my body was fighting back, reminding me that I didn't want to drink. Once I cut back on alcohol, my sugar sensitivity was heightened and when I did drink and the "begats" took over—alcohol begat pizza, begat ice cream, begat more alcohol—it was like I had no willpower. Something I later realized had a different root cause.

As the next month passed, I continued to work on my intention and the connections to my bulimia. There was a link to growing up a sickly child and not wanting to accept it—*never* believing it. A link to all the sleeping around I did after my divorce and "using" my body. What a waste! I sure wasn't there physically for the encounters. It was just my continued search for acceptance.

Letting Go of Family Issues

With each discovery came more understanding and peace. When Henry came home for Thanksgiving

I was so excited to have him home, but I felt bloated and fat and was really emotional. All week I felt I needed to have some time with him to help my healing process.

Henry and I went to dinner over the weekend with my sister Deb and her new beau (she and her first husband divorced). After dinner I started to do the "usual" analyzing of the event with the way my sister acted, what she said. As I was saying this, I (as the witness) heard myself and wondered why I felt it necessary to analyze every family encounter. But then, it was well learned from my mother. She always analyzed encounters with people and always had something to say. This was one of those "a-ha" moments.

The next morning Henry pointed out to me that although I had physically pulled back from my family, mentally I was still all wound up and confused.

"Why don't you just deal with your family issues and let them go?" He also said maybe this was why my stomach was so bloated. I agreed with him, but didn't know exactly what to do to "process" and release the family wounds. He suggested writing.

It took me a couple of days to get through it. But I wrote a couple of pages about each family member. I allowed myself to be totally honest about how I felt and let it be okay that I didn't like some family members, was mad at others, and hurt by others. I always felt this obligatory pressure to love my family and play the part.

Once I allowed myself to speak freely about each family member and let the issues go, my stomach was completely flat, in two days. Wow! That's what I call healing from within!

I knew even before Henry came home I needed to be with him to progress to the next level and now I knew why. All of the pain of being apart was worth it because I was growing so much and he was happy in school building electric guitars! Well, he *had* been, until just before he came home for Thanksgiving—then his attitude changed and everything turned sour grapes. He was unhappy about the grade he received on his first guitar. He was unhappy about how the course was being taught. He was unhappy about… you name it, he was just plain unhappy—*again*. Ugh!

After Henry went back to Phoenix I had my last glass of wine. When I woke the next morning, it was like someone had flipped a switch. I felt like I was up above the clouds after being subjected to cloudy weather for three weeks. The desire to drink was gone. I had my willpower back and was disinterested like when I had quit drinking five years before.

When I went to happy hours or Christmas parties, it was a game to see how I would fend off those who would try and pressure me to drink. What personal power I had found, and what freedom I was enjoying. I slept wonderfully night after night, was committed to my workouts and simply enjoyed the growth and peace that I had found. I finally surrendered to my healing and I was gaining ground that even a month ago felt like it would never arrive.

Forgiveness

To this day, when I stop and think about how I treated myself for the past thirty-four years, I am appalled. How I withheld love from myself, judged myself, and snarled at myself in disgust every time I looked in the mirror. Continually telling myself that I wasn't good enough, I wasn't acceptable, I was fat, and I didn't measure up. That is some pretty brutal karma to look at face-to-face!

From the time I watched *What the Bleep Do We Know!?* and understood that I needed to forgive myself until I was finally able to quit beating up on myself, it was a good five months.

Once I set my intention to be conscious, I still struggled with drinking and bingeing when I didn't want to, but I wasn't beating myself up. Why? Because I knew I was processing. I was frustrated by why I couldn't make it stop and what link I was missing. I was frustrated by how tight my clothes fit and that I wasn't losing any weight. *But* I didn't beat myself up.

This was a journey, as Tina had said, it wouldn't all happen right away. I knew I just needed to surrender to my healing. I needed to quit trying to control the timeline and events.

One of the more intense energy sessions I had was the day I connected with my own Source energy and filled *my* heart with unconditional love. I cried uncontrollably as I felt a flow of beautiful energy fill the void in my heart. The void caused by continually giving to others, but never to myself.

This outpouring of love gave me a new "high." I had a visual of standing on a beach, basking in the sun and feeling the energy feed me. That was *my* connection with Source. It has always been in nature. My visits to the mountains or the ocean were my ticket to slowing down and nourishment. Even back in my Type-A days, I knew that in order to slow down, I had to get away. I found a connection with the universe through nature.

Summary of Progress

✔ Through energy healing I gained a deep understanding of the issues that tied me to bulimia. I released years of stagnant energy that was in my body but no longer needed. I also painfully relived some of my behaviors as we "peeled back the onion."

✔ By watching *What the Bleep Do We Know!?* I was able to understand more about quantum physics and the new concepts I was being introduced to through energy healing.

✔ I discovered the concept of being in the vibrational pattern to attract what we want and setting our intention to create the life we want.

✔ As a result of my energy healing I watched my metamorphosis from bulimic and stressed, to person with balance. I connected with my feminine energy, found a connection to my spiritual self and started to let go of long-held family issues

Chapter 14

Control

*I've learned that you shouldn't go through life
with a catcher's mitt on both hands;
you need to be able to throw something back.*
—Maya Angelou

Life moves and changes quickly. In the midst
of writing this book, the opportunity to move
to California presented itself. Henry was fin-
ishing luthier school and would soon begin a new
career as a guitar repair tech and builder.

HB was never happy in Denver and this unhap-
piness enveloped me in a way I had to change. I
wanted so much to enjoy this man and see him enjoying life vs. moving through day-to-day in a state
of monotonous boredom. Nothing excited him or
really made him happy.

He couldn't find anything that made him feel
connected to his life's passion. But even worse—he
couldn't figure out what he was passionate about at

this point in life. He was always down and focused on why things weren't going the way he wanted them to. He was miserable—and I couldn't deal with the negativity anymore.

Henry kept telling me it was his problem and he would figure it out. But what he didn't understand was how much his issues were affecting me. The connection I felt on his first visit to Denver wasn't there any more. I knew we had more to experience, more to gain, a life we should be enjoying together.

I felt a great deal of uncertainty in how to make the move and continue to enjoy a similar level of income as I'd had in Denver. Much of what made me successful in sales was my Rolodex of clients. I started to search for a new company, and set my intention to find the right opportunity to help us move to California. That was it!

I started interviewing in October and was encouraged by the receptivity I got from California companies—even without a book of business from existing clients.

The Power of Letting Go

In early December, full of frustration for my current employer, I spent a lunch hour parked at a shopping mall. I called everyone I knew and told them I was looking for a way to move to California and that I wanted to do something different.

My friend who co-founded the start-up company I worked for earlier had an idea. She told me to send my resume to her and she would forward it on to three guys who recently started a new company together. She thought I might be a great fit.

I sent my resume at 6:00 the next morning and had a call by 4:00 that afternoon! As I hung up the phone from that first conversation, I asked my higher self, "Is this it?"

I got a very emphatic, "Yes, this is it!"

For the first time, I simply watched the events unfold. I did not stress, I did not try to control. I just watched—because I believed *this* was my new position.

In less than three weeks, I met with all three of the owners and had a job offer with better pay. The timing was perfect. I gave notice to my current employer to leave on December 30 and made plans to start with the new company on January 1. How cool is that?

Starting a new job on January 1 was awesome! The time of year we get a clean slate and a new start. I even managed to get some extra time off during the holidays to enjoy Henry while he was home from school.

I had just discovered a whole new way of living through stressful times. Instead of being afraid that something might happen and I wouldn't get the job offer, or thinking through all the worst-case scenarios, I *trusted* and let the universe lead me to the answer.

This change led to many "unknowns." I would have to practice my new tools and learn to stay patient. For starters I had agreed to join my new company in the position of project manager for three months to get an in-depth view of our business and get to know the client, Warner Bros. (WB) before taking on my sales role. WB was one of my new company's largest clients. This meant I would travel to Los Angeles every week and work on the lot at WB. Henry was still in Phoenix and I had two dogs at home. I wasn't thrilled about traveling again, but it was a means to an end.

I continued to exercise my new tools to deal with stressful situations. When I was headed to the airport and it looked like there was no way in hell I would make my flight, I didn't stress out. Hey, I was either going to make the flight or not, and if I didn't make the flight, the next one would be there shortly and I would be on it. Interesting thing is, every time I thought I *might* miss my flight something happened and I made it.

I discovered a new way to interact with the events of daily living—without spending a great deal of energy getting frustrated, worrying or tensing up! I could *feel* the difference, my massage therapist could tell the difference—and I was sleeping much better.

I started working with a personal trainer to get in shape for the upcoming vacation Henry and I had scheduled to Hawaii after he finished school. In two months I was able to get back to 115 pounds and into most of my clothes. After two weeks in Maui, I put the house up for sale.

Excuse Me, Your Life Is Waiting

Toward the end of the year while I was interviewing and looking for my new job I was also reading a great book called, *Excuse Me, Your Life is Waiting* by Lynn Grabhorn. This book is similar to the *Ask* book and concentrated on *feeling* vs. just thinking positive or using affirmations to help you attract what you want in life. This created an interesting challenge for me as feeling isn't something that I was used to doing. But I experimented over and over, tried many of her suggestions and found them to be very resourceful.

I wanted to sell the house by myself and was led to all the channels that made it easy for that to happen.

At the beginning of the year, Henry and I set an intention to find our new home in California. People thought I was nuts, but I was *vibrating* for a home that:

◇ Was 3,000 square feet in the greater Los Angeles area

✧ Had a large kitchen with a center island
✧ Had a large yard for the dogs
✧ Had a three-car garage
✧ Had room for my gym (my basement in Denver was my gym)
✧ Had space for my office
✧ Had space for Henry's studio
✧ Had a quiet street with friendly neighbors
✧ Had an affordable mortgage
✧ Achieved by June 30, 2006

Everyone knows you can't find a yard in Southern California and if you do it will be a multi-million dollar home!

I sent the brochure of my home in Denver to everyone I could think of. I held open houses and even found a way to get listed in MLS for a flat fee!

Right after I listed on MLS I got a call from one of my clients. She was thinking about buying my home as an investment. Wow! She and her husband already owned several properties out of state and wanted some properties in Colorado.

My brother suggested I keep the house as an investment myself. This led to a connection with a person whose business was to find people who were looking for "lease to own" homes. The path was intriguing!

I looked at houses in LA a couple of times. Henry moved to LA in March, was working as a guitar repair tech and making some great connections for himself. We decided to wait to look at houses until there was more momentum in Denver.

The Power of Intention

Things seemed to be moving slowly, Henry was in LA, the dogs were terribly lonely being left with a pet sitter three to four days every week and I was tired of traveling. I wanted us to be back together again. So, I set my intention for the house to sell.

Then it hit me, perhaps I was doing this all wrong? I told Henry we should make an appointment to look at houses in California and maybe that would *create* the momentum for the house to sell. We made an appointment to house shop the next Monday. On Sunday the day before I left for California I got an offer on my house! This intention-setting stuff really works!

The next day we saw eight houses I found on www.Realtor.com and put an offer on our new home. Standing in the yard I had a feeling of solace. It was *almost* an exact fit with the goals we set earlier in the year. The house:

✧ Was 2,230 square feet vs. 3,000
✧ Had a medium-sized kitchen, but no center island
✧ Had a large yard for the dogs only 100 square feet smaller than our yard in Denver

- ✧ Had a three-car garage
- ✧ Had a loft for my gym which was larger than my basement in Denver
- ✧ Had space for my office, with a view of the backyard waterfall
- ✧ Had space for Henry's studio—he had two rooms to choose from
- ✧ Had a quiet street with friendly neighbors—it was on a cul-de-sac
- ✧ Had an affordable mortgage
- ✧ We got possession of the home June 13, before my June 30 deadline.

Now *that's* what I call attracting what you focus on! It had only been three weeks since I set my intention to sell the house, *and* the house we bought had only been on the market for one week. I was amazed at how well I was learning to control stress, and at how calm I was able to stay through all the unknowns. By letting go, by letting everything be okay and not trying to control everything, my life was changing in quantum leaps. I was effortlessly creating how I wanted my life to be.

With a history of bulimia and a strong need to control each and every little thing, this was nothing short of spectacular!

There is freedom in letting go of control. The reduction of stress in my life was a welcome change!

Henry noticed how different I was dealing with stress than even six months earlier. I too noticed differences in my behavior as I responded to making plans with people. Instead of trying to have everything mapped out and each detail defined, I was becoming a "let's wait and see," or "let's plan it when we get there" person.

I liked the flexibility of this approach. Now it was time to pack, plan the move and make all the arrangements to get us to California.

Summary of Progress

✔ I learned the power of letting go by continuing to practice the new concepts I was learning in bigger, more stressful situations (being late for a flight, finding a new job).

✔ I learned to trust my gut instead of stressing about everything.

✔ Through *Excuse Me, Your Life Is Waiting* I learned a practical approach to create and manifest the situations I wanted by *feeling*. A huge step for a recovering bulimic!

✔ I continued to step out of my comfort zone and used my intention to sell my home in Denver and locate the right new home in So Cal.

Chapter 15

Little Lori and the Move

What makes something special is not just what you have to gain, but what you feel there is to lose.
—Andre Agassi

I should have known that all the activities related to moving were going to stir up some shit. The thought of packing the entire house alone combined with juggling three upcoming business trips was daunting. Sales were heating up with the new job. Great news, but how would I do it all?

But I felt surprisingly calm while planning for all of these changes. Long-time friends couldn't believe how calm I was.

Traveling every week for four months had made it difficult to maintain my usual workout schedule. Once again, being vegan and traveling made it even worse. It's hard to find healthy food and protein. And eating five small meals a day was an even bigger challenge.

I was working sixty-five to seventy hours a week. There were days I got a quick breakfast and then didn't get to eat again until 8:30 or 9:00 at night. Going without food was the worst thing I could do, being sugar sensitive. I often ended up at the hotel starving, with only pasta or potatoes to choose from on the menu—the last thing I needed at 9:00 at night. I wanted my workouts, I wanted to eat *my* way and I wanted to cut back on my drinking and get my body back.

As I started working in LA I picked up the vibe that my wardrobe was too conservative. I felt pressure to step up. Moving to So Cal I felt I could be a little more "LA" and a little less corporate. A thought likely shaped from working on the lot at WB.

I went shopping and bought a new wardrobe. Yeah—at a point when I needed every penny to pay for the move, I bought a new wardrobe! But I got a bonus that covered it. I found some really cool stuff at Nordstrom's and although I was up a few pounds, they were still size 4s and I could tell when I got back to my normal weight they would be perfect. This was about a month before the move. Okay, new clothes, new city, new life, I set my intention to be sober for six months.

Loss of Control—Helplessness

The next thing I knew I was drinking like a fish! I ate pizza with cheese at the airport twice because

I was starving and there was *nothing* else to eat *and* I ate more pizza at home on the weekend.

My body started to expand. I felt a huge loss of control over my eating, my schedule and workouts. There were days I left Denver in the wee morning hours, flew to a meeting in California and returned late at night. The frustration got to me. I was back to the old bulimic tapes of "What the hell, I've already blown it..."

The last thing I wanted to do was move to LA and weigh more than I had in four years! LA is the "look perfect" capital. Yeah, my weight had been up and down a little with the colon cleanse and Candida in the previous couple of years, but I felt awful!

I tried to keep my focus off my weight and how I looked. I bought some hip-looking jeans that had 2% polyester so I could still fit in them when I felt gross. A truly ingenuous idea! This was to keep me away from my tendency to wear my baggy carpenter jeans when I felt fat.

But the final two weeks before the move I was completely out of control. I met with Tina and discovered something I hadn't even considered. Little Lori, my inner child, was really freaking out. When I had moved to Denver from Chicago I said I wasn't going to move again. She was trying to hold me to it!

During the course of the healing session we found that most of the unrest, eating and drinking was caused by a fear coming from deep down inside.

Tina encouraged me to spend some time with Little Lori and assure her that everything would be okay. She also suggested that once I arrived in the new house I take the time to give Little Lori a tour of the place, acquaint her with everything, make her comfortable, let her know this was our new home and everything was all right.

This one blew me over—how can we be so blind to the obvious? How could I have made all these plans, and felt so calm only to find out that I was falling apart inside?

My Ear

In my last session with Tina before I moved, the energy in my right ear surfaced. It was almost a year to the day that I first went to see her about it. This energy was convinced I couldn't make it alone, without it there to block things out for me. I was able to let the old energy go. This was so cool—coming full circle before I left!

Weight Gain "R" Us

As it turned out, the weight gain I had *before* the move was NOTHING! Once we arrived in our new home there were a host of issues. Many things the previous owners had not maintained that needed to be fixed and new things that needed to be purchased. I had no intention of spending money I didn't have. But in two months I overspent by several thousand dollars and was freaked out about how I would pay for it. Not that it was a horrific amount of money—but I don't like carrying debt.

So the money; the fact that Henry and I, finally back together, were greatly disconnected; Alta, my Samoyed, almost fourteen, wasn't handling the move well or adjusting to the new house; along with feeling fat and scared—all sent me into a huge tailspin.

I made the discovery of inexpensive Sangria table wine at the local grocery store. It wasn't as potent as the wine I usually drank and I could drink a whole quart for $4.99!

I drank almost every day. There were a few days I even drank while I worked. I ate entire bags of tortilla chips or an eight-ounce bag of almonds in one sitting. I couldn't seem to get control.

Every day that I drank, my whole body swelled up. This had been happening for a while, but if I held it to one or two glasses of wine, I didn't swell as much.

The first month in California was chaos. It took us three weeks to get the boxes unpacked, get my weight machines back together, my gym set up and finish painting in an attempt to feel like we lived in our new home. Yet, the house felt so strange.

I got the nerve to get on the scale to see how bad it was; I weighed 124! I hadn't been anywhere near that weight since '01 before I did EAS. I was horrified.

I worked from home and initially most days I didn't have to get dressed and go anywhere. So while I ballooned, I wasn't in touch with how bad it had gotten except the days I had meetings with clients. I was aghast at how my clothing fit (or didn't) and mortified when I had to leave the house.

Yet, it continued. I just couldn't seem to find a way to make it stop. Here I was, *finally* in a situation where I could work out, eat *my* food, on *my* schedule, have the family back together and I had completely lost it.

I hadn't vibrated the move to be anything like this. I envisioned this push to the finish, followed by happiness, and "solace." Instead, Henry and I were at odds and he was back to the same old "just not happy, didn't know why." I couldn't take it any more. I was paying for *everything* because the income from his new career was coming in slowly and all he did was complain that things didn't *feel* right. My level of frustration was through the roof.

Feng Shui

One day I read an article in a local magazine written by a Feng Shui consultant, Elaine Giftos Wright. She mentioned several things in her article that really caught my eye. Elaine described homes with Feng Shui issues or imbalance, these included homes on a cul-de-sac, homes with stairs in the middle of the house…Our house was in a cul-de-sac, our stairs were in the middle of the house, and many, many things had gone wrong since we arrived. I felt like I was living in the movie *The Money Pit*!

Elaine's article talked about how she helped a client transform her life from one where everything was falling apart to being totally "back on track," all from making some Feng Shui adjustments. Henry was up for it, so I called.

Feng Shui tied right in with my philosophy of setting intention, goals and visualization. How cool was that?

I told Elaine about my health issues from the previous two years—I wasn't sure why I was sharing it with her, but I found out this could be affected by the energy in the home. We had to make changes in the "chi," or center of the home, that were specifically designed to help my health, poor digestion and eliminate the drinking.

Other things were wrong with our home, but with Feng Shui "cures" they could all be fixed. I got all of these "cures" and ended up spending a lot more money! At the time it felt painful, but it was cheaper than moving out of a poorly designed home and environment.

Some of the cures were wonderful; she asked me to get a water fountain for the front of the house, which would invite abundance, wealth for our careers and healing for my ear.

Elaine suggested we run the water fountain in the backyard all the time to encourage abundance. More money! The water fountain wasn't running well and we had to hire someone to help us clean it out. I felt like I was hemorrhaging money.

A few days later I woke up with an idea about the debt. When I called one of my credit cards that I hadn't used in several years they offered me an interest-free cash advance for nine months. I could easily pay off the debt by then! I felt such relief—I had found an answer that would allow me to let go of the fear all the debt created. I found an answer and now I could relax about the finances.

Back to My Healing

I continued to work with Tina long distance. I had completely shut down my healing during the move. I was back trying to control everything and had forgotten about surrender and unconditional love. I kept saying, "Why am I so swollen, this isn't even my body, when will it stop?" I was reminded that what I needed to do once again was accept myself where I was in order to heal. Difficult words to hear when you are 14 pounds overweight!

My confidence was shaken. I was worried I would get in trouble because I wasn't working as much as I should be—yet the deals and connections were starting to come.

The day I started to surrender and give myself unconditional love, I felt the healing return. It was slow at first.

Tina assured me that I hadn't lost ground and was still okay. Only the loop of the "behavior" had expanded. We spoke about how much stress there was with the move and how I had kept it all in check. But the stress and uncertainty of the new digs, city and job, combined with the huge disconnect from Henry felt like my undoing.

Now that I was allowing myself a little down time I was exhausted and had no energy. When the weekends came I was on the couch cheering Tiger Woods on, but alas not *doing* anything. It didn't feel good, where had all my energy gone? Why couldn't I write? I wanted to golf so badly, but didn't know a soul to golf with and hadn't found the strength to venture out on my own.

One day, after I drank a bottle and a half of wine, followed by a glass of Sangria and slept through my massage appointment, I knew I had to do something. I woke up bloated, with a headache, and my ear was completely plugged up. I listed out what happened when I drank:

✧ I become unconscious—the opposite direction I wanted to go

✧ I consume extra calories (carbs)
✧ My body swells up—an allergic reaction?
✧ My ear plugs up—an allergic reaction or just a message?
✧ It lowers my vibration

This wasn't the path I wanted to follow! I questioned whether ego was the reason I continued to experience the sabotage from my old behaviors.

I set new goals, made new cards with my intentions that I read and visualized morning and night.

A week later, it hit me...I was completely focused on the *wrong* thing! I was continually writing affirmations about being sober, which kept me focused on drinking. Our subconscious can't decipher a negative, whatever we think is taken as a command. I realized that drinking, just like food, wasn't my issue and that writing a zillion affirmations and goals about my fitness and goal weight and what I eat or drink wasn't going to help me. I needed to create affirmations about how to deal with and express my emotions!

I had to accept that my bulimic issues were very deep and the more we dig, the more we "peel the onion," the more we find. I wasn't bulimic for over thirty years because of little things. I needed to surrender to my healing. There was something very deep and apparently very dark that continued to hold me.

I set some new intentions. The first were:

✧ I am living my life in the present.
✧ I am increasing my level of consciousness and vibration every day.

Then I created the affirmations I needed to erase some poor beliefs and create some better focus for me:

✧ I am eating and enjoying a large variety of foods. My high metabolism efficiently processes whatever I eat. I am healthy, energetic and thriving!
✧ I am dealing with, processing and express-ing my emotions in ways that are healthy for me!

Now *this* felt like a quantum leap! I felt like I was *finally* addressing the root cause and not the symptom.

I had been marking my workout calendar with a " + " for every day I didn't drink. I decided to stop. Tracking good days put too much focus to the act of drinking, and scorecards weren't what I needed right now.

I looked back at my EAS food journal to see if there was anything I did differently that I had forgot-ten and there *was*. My diet had shifted so significantly during the Candida fight that I had gotten into a real rut of what I could and couldn't eat. On EAS I was eating more fresh fruit and raw veggies, and there were no notes about full jars of almonds!

I started to find positives in little places. I realized I had already sold more than my sales quota for the year and it was only August! As soon as we cleaned the water fountain in the backyard and got it running I got three high-level referrals from one of my clients. Henry said he was finally starting to feel some optimism. We were experiencing a shift! The Feng Shui cures were working.

With the move I had fallen hard, I had relapsed. Something I didn't expect. I thought I had grown beyond this. What I learned was there was still more healing to process, more energy to move, more issues to deal with.

Learning to Express Emotions

After setting my affirmations about my expressing my emotions, two things happened that brought me to new and *very* uncomfortable experiences. The first wasn't a huge thing. One day, after three months of fighting with the phone company over a credit I was supposed to get now because our carrier shifted from one company to another I was told there was no record of the credit. My morning had already been stressful. I let out a yell and really let myself get angry...and stayed there until it passed. I didn't like how tight I felt inside. I could feel my body enraged with anger. Is this what I'm hiding when I run from my feelings all the time? Wow!

The second thing happened a little later in the week and was just a sudden rise of "feelings." While out running errands I became agitated, felt a headache coming on. Once home Alta was begging insistently and wouldn't lie down while I fixed dinner. I couldn't put my finger on anything specific, but I was all worked up—angry and full of frustration.

By the time I sat down to eat I was in tears. Again, my body was writhing in anger; I felt so tight inside and realized if this is what I do while I'm numb it can't be good for me. I stayed in it, ate my dinner and realized about thirty minutes later that it had passed and I was over it.

Both of these situations were *so* incredibly uncomfortable for me. Feeling this anger, feeling this frustration, feeling something that wasn't pleasant, feeling irritable and letting it out—not a place I'm used to being. But I made it through consciously, without alcohol.

After the second experience I knew I could continue on this path. This was the growth I needed because many times I would feel frustrated. Usually when it happened I wasn't even sure where it came from, but I ran to the bottle so I didn't have to know—didn't have to find out.

Alta finally started to settle down and use the

dog door. Things were getting better. Could it have been my energy, my unrest that caused hers?

Digging Deep

In my next energy session I found out that even though I had processed a lot I was just now going to hit the deeper stuff. I was headed for more challenging work. In preparation for it I needed to get my emotions out of me and down on paper. This process and what I had been experiencing would cause chaos in my system. Everything up until then was prep work for deeper, raw spiritual work. GREAT! Kind of scary, and yet, if this is what it was going to take to move beyond the chains that were holding me, I was ready.

I wanted to learn to manifest on a larger level. Tina said this would involve surrendering to the outcome, without angst, without demanding, without panic, and without emotionally blackmailing the universe.

Sometimes we don't manifest what we want because there is a positive lesson we need to learn or because we aren't ready to receive the manifestation yet. I had to remember there is beauty in the *process.*

I still had many issues tied to not loving myself and these affected my heart and my gut. The concept of self-love was important for me because I withheld it from myself for so long. Going through life hating what you see in the mirror doesn't flood your soul with love and appreciation!

I had huge anger tied to control. A great deal of it was feeling mislead in my childhood. I felt like *my* power had been taken away from me. Wow! I had been feeling a lot of anger in the last month, which wasn't typical for me.

The Blame Game

Four days later Alta died. I was at a lunch with a client at the time. She wasn't acting herself that morning so I had made an appointment to take her to the vet when I got home. I got the car ready, ran to get her and found her lying beside the house, eyes open. I couldn't believe it!

Once it set in, I was bawling my eyes out. I had tried to prepare myself for this day since she was three, but there was no way to prepare for the suddenness of her departure.

Alta was my first kid. We had been through so much together. I wondered if the move caused it. Had I made the wrong decision? Should I have taken her to the vet instead of going to my lunch meeting?

I called the vet to cancel the appointment and she told me there was likely nothing they could have done if Alta went that quickly. I was consumed with guilt.

I recognized that something Henry pointed out to me on a few occasions was interestingly true: I am *always* ready to take on the blame in a situation and evaluate what I did wrong or how I caused it. Always *so* willing to point the finger at myself and then worry about being in trouble.

When I went to bed I knew I had to let go of the guilt. Her death wasn't my fault; she would have been fourteen in three weeks. She had lived a long life.

The next day as I thought about it I realized she stayed around long enough to get me through the move. If Yager had been alone while I was traveling every week he would have been a mess. I saw that she stayed long enough to get us to So Cal and was ready to go. It was *so* painful!

I woke up in tears for several days knowing she wouldn't be outside doing her little right-to-left foot prancing, waiting for her breakfast when I came down. Okay, so someone was trying to push the envelope and make me feel things—I get it!

Five days later on my way to meet some of my consultants for dinner I was in a car accident on the freeway. The cars had slowed to gape at an over-turned truck on the other side of the road and were starting to accelerate. Suddenly I let out a scream as I realized the driver in front of me was stopped again and I was going to hit her. I was in the Rocket, the car I got through goal setting!

I was completely out of it after the accident. The

airbags deployed and scared the crap out of me. I thought the car was on fire from the smoke, which I learned later came from what they use to pack the airbags.

I couldn't figure out how this happened, I'm a great driver, I have a clean driving record and I was listening to my Lynn Grabhorn CDs and focused on being positive. The law of attraction says when accidents happen our focus is what causes them. What negativity was I focused on to cause this? I started to worry about my insurance rates going up; I worried about getting my car fixed…and then realized…I was worried about being in trouble again. Why?

I did some journaling a few days later and asked:

Why am I always so afraid that I'm in trouble? I am not a bad person. Where is the root of this and how can I let it go?

I also asked for the answer why I was sitting on the couch, night after night falling asleep. Wine or no wine, I zonked out. I even made a list of things I could do in the evening based on my level of energy. Life was passing me by while I slept on the couch.

Henry and I were not in a good place. Over the past two months I had started to question our relationship and whether we should stay together. As I wrote I found a whole lot of anger. Anger at Henry, anger at the way our situation had turned out, anger at all of his disinterest in life, in never being happy, in letting me down from the dreams we made that first Christmas. I was angry and hurt. It was painful to realize and *consciously* accept that I had such strong negative feelings toward him.

I talked with Tina about all the unrest, the blame and guilt I was feeling. She sensed I had some really big stuff going on and said I was clearing out space at a rapid rate. This was why I was feeling all dis-combobulated (that's a technical term!). I was in the process of moving from things I "know" and it felt uncomfortable. I was getting ready to create new things. I needed to sit and get information from my higher self on what I wanted to create and manifest.

We found a lot of issues connected to my child-hood. Blame was something my mom had used to keep me in check through fear. (It obviously worked!) There were issues tied to being in trouble with my dad. I saw how my mom manipulated him and felt betrayed when he disciplined me because she told him to.

Tina and I talked about all the "blame." I was blaming myself, denying part of myself an existence. I had so much blame *and* fear. She said a lot of the blame I was placing on Henry was mirroring. When I let go of blaming myself, I would probably lighten up on him.

I started drinking more. Henry and I weren't getting along *at all*. I felt awful and couldn't figure out where all this sabotage was coming from. While journaling, it hit me: Could I even envision what my life would be like without bulimia? What is that vision? What is my life *like*? What is *normal*? I made a list of fifteen changes that included:

- ✧ Sleeping well *every* night
- ✧ Having energy *every* morning and on weekends
- ✧ Deciding what to wear based on mood and occasion vs. what I can fit into
- ✧ Loving my life and my body
- ✧ Living life at peace with wonderful energy flow, happiness, vitality and confidence

Wow, this felt good! Why hadn't I thought of painting this picture before? I had always tried to find the positive spin on things, but I missed this one—until now.

Summary of Progress

✔ With the move I experienced a huge relapse from all the stress. I lost my grounding and gained 12 pounds.

✔ With Feng Shui I was able to clear out the negative energy that was in our home and found a connection with the other concepts I was using to live my life (intention, visualization).

✔ After a year and a half of energy healing I started to be able to stay in the moment and deal with my emotions and feel what anger did to my body.

✔ I started to focus and visualize my life free of bulimia. And concentrated on how that would *feel*.

✔ I found that blame and my fear of being in trouble was a root cause of some significant thought processes and subsequent responses in life.

✔ I made the connection to create affirmations to help me express my emotions.

Chapter 16

❧

Finding Consciousness and Peace

Life is really simple, but we insist on making it complicated.
—Confucius

The next day when I journaled, I was back in touch with my sugar sensitivity and decided I had to go back and study it again. I reread most of *Potatoes Not Prozac*, which brought me answers about lack of energy and motivation—about why I was on the couch all the time.

The first time I read *Potatoes Not Prozac*, I was doing my EAS Challenge and several of Kathleen's suggestions were already part of my lifestyle. I had read the paragraph about the effects of alcohol on a sugar-sensitive person but didn't try to change my behavior. Back then I was constantly looking for someone, or something, to tell me I had to stop drinking, even though I didn't want to. It was such a pleasant crutch, but I hated it.

Now, my desire for balance and peace and the need to remove myself from the roller coaster outweighed everything else. I realized the issues Kathleen discussed in her book were what contributed to my current situation. It wasn't self-sabotage—but sugar. My sugar sensitivity was *so* strong that I had to continue to watch my intake. Funny, I had just finished Martina Navratilova's new book, *Shape Your Self,* the week before and started to make fresh fruit juice, which she does daily. Little did I know that would contribute to a binge I had a week later!

Reading about the sugar sensitivity really helped center me, it brought me such a feeling of calm.

Exit the Sugar Train

In journaling I saw the pattern. I would typically get a bottle of wine on Friday, which was when I enjoyed my "free meal." We called it junk-food-Friday night. It was actually not junk food, just Tater Tots and soy chicken nuggets, but more carbs than I ate during the week, and wine. This resulted in a huge blood sugar crash that arrived on Saturday morning—just in time for the weekend. Hello!

I was also exhausted from the move that followed five months of traveling to and from LA. But now I had optimism! I had just discovered the exit to the ride and was getting off the roller coaster.

I started to journal my food intake with my physical and emotional feelings as the book suggested. After just three days I felt much better. I was sleeping more soundly and had energy during the day.

Yager and I started walking three to four times a week in the early evening, which helped my overall energy level and seemed to calm him down. But, I had an awful time waking up in the morning even with seven to eight hours of sleep. This shifted after two weeks and I started to wake up before the alarm. My energy was much higher, I felt more balance and felt the relief of the sugar overload. As I looked back I saw all the chemical contributions to what had happened. I wrote:

"During this year I was totally out of control from the way I wanted to eat—that was following two years of huge frustration from the Candida issues, special diets, adrenal fatigue and the colon cleanse. All these things that took away what I found with EAS.

"Now I had found the plug that activates the roller coaster—the plug that needs to stay unplugged! I am feeling peace, and yes, I will vibrate and continue my affirmations and intention to remove the sugar sensitivity, but for now I have found the exit from the ride, that 'Ah'."

Two Steps Forward...

I had started golfing when I got into sales and found I had an aptitude for it. I loved being outdoors, enjoyed the aesthetics of each golf course and challenging myself to improve my handicap. I played a lot entertaining clients and was lucky enough to gain some golf buddies with some of my male clients. We often golfed even when it wasn't work related. This year I had only golfed on vacation, in Hawaii in February and once before we moved. I missed it. I usually used to play thirty to forty times a year.

I finally went one weekend and found I could actually still play after five months! When I was done, my brain wanted the "after golf drink." I came home and had one glass of red wine. And that was it. No bingeing, nothing. This was cool! I had *definitely* found the answer.

I continued my food journal, but during the next week wasn't drinking much water. I didn't have my usual supply of raw vegetables to chew on while I was working, and missed some meals because of work demands—priming my blood sugar for the sugar choo-choo.

HB and I had our biggest fight ever over the weekend followed by two days that were emotionally unsettling. So a couple of days after the golf drink, I decided to have another drink—just one glass, because I knew I could do it. I was in control.

Two days later the binge hit. It wasn't a huge one, but it made me swell up again. But *this* time I had been in witness mode the whole time. I watched the entire behavior unfold. I saw that it was way too early in the process for me to experiment with wine two to three times in one week. Plus, this was defeating the purpose of what I was trying to do: remove sugar from my system and lose weight.

I was confused why I was still dozing off in the evening. I tried reading one night, and started to nod about 9:45. I tried listening to a course I was taking on my computer the next night and started to doze again around 9:45. I tried to watch a movie the next night, same result.

Thankfully, after awakening to the fact that I experimented a little too much—my energy level shifted again, this time for the better.

Greens?

I read a book called *Green For Life*. An interesting new concept. In this book, Victoria Boutenko relates her family's struggle with disease that led them to a raw food diet. The *Green* book came about because after several years on a raw diet Victoria was experiencing issues with some raw foods—especially salads—so she started eating mostly fruits and nuts. She realized that her family was not eating enough greens (mainly because they didn't like them) and decided to study the diet of chimpanzees to determine what quantities of greens they ate.

Victoria's book details her study of chimp eating habits. Through her study she found that to release all the valuable nutrients from within the cells of a green, the cells needed to be "ruptured." Humans can't chew our greens long enough to get them to the state needed to fully gain the benefit of wonderful vitamins, minerals and other nutrients they have. She decided to make green smoothies in a blender.

Within a couple of months she noticed significant changes in the way she felt and in her skin. Most notably she wasn't craving food any more. Wow! Could this be the ultimate answer I had been waiting for?

As I continued to read I found to my delight that these green smoothies *were* the answer to the soy protein issue I had been contemplating since reading *The Mood Cure* a couple of years ago. "Greens provide protein in the form of individual amino acids. These amino acids are easier for the body to utilize than complex proteins. A variety of greens can supply all the protein we need to sustain each of our unique bodies."[1] Cool! I had been looking for a way to stop using the manufactured soy proteins (Morningstar foods, Worthington Foods, Loma Linda Foods). My goal was to use as little processed food as possible in my diet.

Victoria talked about the body's ability to heal itself if given the right fuel. Something I believe.

With greens you can support the process of homeostasis, and support your entire health better than any other food. Greens provide such a power pack of nutrients: vitamins, amino acids—this was tying back to my studies about endocrinology a couple of years earlier. Way cool!

Victoria also has a chapter on the significance of stomach acid and symptoms that occur when people don't have the amount they need. Been there, done that, she was preaching to the choir!

Greens make our bodies more alkaline and help maintain the balance. Greens provide healing through chlorophyll. Victoria included many personal stories of individuals who were using the green shakes. These were powerful stories of changes in lifestyle, more energy, moles disappearing, hair returning to its original color (from gray), and more.

I got a combination of fruits and vegetables and started to make green smoothies. They weren't bad. I especially liked the amount I could consume because I was drinking greens vs. chewing. There is no possible way I could eat as many greens, fruits and veggies as I was consuming in the shakes.

After a couple of weeks I felt different when I woke up. I felt clarity, focus, a clearer brain. I had an interest in work and was able to re-engage. This was awesome!

I waited for the cravings to stop. But now I found myself craving sugar *intensely*. I didn't understand it, but I did feel better drinking the shakes so I continued. Around the fourth week I had lunch with a client at a wonderful Italian restaurant in Burbank. We had appetizers, white bread, pasta and a couple of glasses of wine (it was Friday). After I left my client's office I stopped in Starbucks for some decaf and ordered a pumpkin scone. Huh? Where did *that* come from?

The next day I figured it out. I was consuming massive quantities of sugar from the fruit in the green smoothies. I have never liked honeydew, but I tried it in the shakes and it was good, so I made it several times. I was using grapes and bananas—high sugar content fruits. Duh!

So, I started to make smoothies using only vegetables and on occasion added blueberries or strawberries. It relieved my cravings somewhat, but I was still having a strong pull for wine once or twice a week. I was feeling better and thought I was losing a little weight so I stuck with it. I felt like I was close… but didn't yet have the "final answer." I was *so* tired of it.

The Holidays

Henry and I were having some deep conversations. I noticed I didn't even feel an attraction to him anymore. When I looked at him I felt nothing. Had I simply fallen out of love with him? The more I journaled, the more I was convinced I wanted out. I just had to figure out the right time to tell him. He didn't have money to go and get a place of his own. Not that it was my problem, but the holidays were fast approaching and I just didn't feel it was time to tell him yet. I wanted to be sure, before I took such a big step. In the back of my mind I wondered if I just had an aversion to being in a relationship more than five years. We were coming on the five-year mark and I had split with both Thurston and Rowdy at five years.

I continued to feel negativity from his attitude, which had become such a strong turnoff for me, and I was done. I truly felt this was the answer and even thought that maybe the reason I couldn't get the weight off was because of Henry. If I lost weight and started looking and feeling good, then I wouldn't have any excuses for my lack of intimacy.

This was my mindset as Thanksgiving and our fifth anniversary approached. Thanksgiving: the day that we spend cooking a gourmet vegan feast together enjoying each other's company and the fruits of our labor. Great.

I was pretty withdrawn on Thanksgiving. We cooked, enjoyed some great food, had the neighbors over for dessert and pretended things weren't as bad as they were. It was a miserable day.

With the help of the green smoothies I continued to gain focus. I read three books and the ideas started to flow. I found myself wanting to work on my book again; it had been months.

Since starting on the shakes my whole "diet" changed. I get full quickly and when I would drink my green shake first thing in the morning, I wasn't hungry until several hours later. Then I couldn't decide what to eat. Since reading the book I had this question in my head about going to a raw diet. I wasn't sure I was ready to commit to raw food, but I kept having this feeling in my head that I "should."

I had a couple binges that seemed to come un-provoked by sugar and when I analyzed it I noticed that I wasn't eating very much. The shakes were fill-ing me up so much that I wasn't getting enough *other* food in me and my blood sugar was going whack again.

Ever since I quit food binges I cannot *stand* to be full. I don't eat till I'm full and very rarely over-eat; it's now a feeling I loathe.

I decided to go back to my normal breakfast of oatmeal and use the smoothie for my between-meal snack. Once I did this, the blood sugar balance was much better. But I was still caught in the wine drink-ing. Was it the sugar train or sabotage? I was analyzing it to death and trying to deal with it through willpower.

I decided it was time to locate someone in LA that I could meet in person to continue my energy work. As life always does, I was led, via the Internet, to Susanna Horton. She studied at the same school that Tina's teacher did and knew him—they had been in the same class.

Susanna also practiced acupuncture and did a combination session of energy healing and acupuncture. From our first conversation I felt an instant connection with her.

I was in such a state of indecision, so angry and ready to be alone. I knew Susanna would be able to help me answer these questions and I was preparing to finally be alone in my house. I even knew what color I would repaint Henry's studio. Yeah, that's what I thought going *in*.

The Awakening

The first topic I discussed with Susanna was Henry. She drew a chart from 1% to 100% to see if Henry and I still had potential to be life partners. While I was anticipating the answer that would set me free, I watched the pendulum continue to swing closer and closer to 100%. Not the answer I expected!

Susanna said it would take a year to a year and a half for Henry to reach the point in his career at which I wanted him to be financially. I just needed to be patient. Talk about humbling...okay, I would wait. I guess it wasn't about emancipation this time. HB was a good man and perhaps I had just gotten too focused on what *I* wanted. I wasn't saying it was all good, but I would give it a try.

The second answer I got from Susanna was on the raw diet. She said I needed warm soups and broths to help restore the hole in my Chi energy. A raw food diet was not what I needed to heal. I had a yin deficiency. My hormones were all out of whack because I was in perimenopause. She also thought I was fighting Candida *Again*?

I couldn't believe my ears, Candida! But then it all made sense. The wine cravings, the lack of energy, with all the drinking I did after we moved, of course! And I wasn't still struggling with *bulimia*. The sugar train was closely tied to the flux of Candida in my system. That's why I had no control. Big duh!

So it was back to probiotics, a Candida diet and cleansing my system from the nasty bacteria. I couldn't believe I hadn't connected these dots. Guess I was in living on a river in Egypt (denial).

The last thing Susanna and I discussed was the pumpkin scone I'd had the week earlier. She said my inner child was asking, "What about me?" I hadn't been doing anything for fun. My life of late was all pretty miserable. I had been in serious analytical mode with the questions about Henry and the raw diet and was all wound up. I felt huge relief as I left my healing session. I had found a wonderful new resource in So Cal.

The next time I saw Susanna, she suggested that I stop my aerobics. She said it was too much for my immune system. Susanna had also mentioned that I should consider changing my workouts from morning to later in the day and use the early morning as creative time when I first met with her, but I hadn't started it yet. I was still running sprints three times a week and loved it because I was done in twenty minutes. Granted I wasn't losing any weight, but you can't lose weight when you are drinking a bottle of wine once or twice a week.

Susanna taught me two meditations. One was a heart meditation, the other was for balance and connection with higher self. She felt I needed to spend some time in meditation to get to the next level spiritually. She told me that all the tools I needed to write my book and start my new career were there, waiting for me. I left feeling so enlightened, so blessed!

My sessions with Susanna had a higher spiritual connection, a whole different level of energy and healing. I was indeed getting ready to move to another level, I could feel it.

I left for Denver right after my session. I didn't really want to go, but my company wanted me to come for the Christmas party. When I left I felt awesome. My jeans fit better, I didn't feel embarrassed and I was looking forward to seeing some of my family.

But this trip turned out to be my undoing. I had ice cream, missed meals and drank too much decaf the next day. I wound up eating not one, but *two* desserts at the Christmas party! When I got to my hotel I ate the crap that was in the goody bag.

The next day I flew out early for a meeting in San Francisco, no breakfast, and no time for lunch. By dinner the conductor on the sugar train had my seat warmed up for me. I had a garden burger and sweet potato fries with two Irish coffees at the airport. When I reached home late that night I felt disgusting. I was swollen, full and sugar overdosed. I was just getting grounded again and flying 35,000 feet above the ground had pulled the rug out from under me. I had lost my grounding.

Yoga

Once home, I went in search of a traditional yoga class. The guidance as always was there and I found an awesome yoga center about fifteen minutes from home. I went for an initial evaluation and was happy to find the classes were half stretching and half breathing. The headmaster explained that our breath can be very healing and after evaluating me said I would find significant healing there.

I liked the fact that classes were sixty minutes instead of the typical ninety. *And* it wasn't full of a bunch of poses that I couldn't perform because of my lack of flexibility. I felt inspired after my initial evaluation.

    ❧ ❧ ❧

I was in a really angry place when I arrived for my next session with Susanna. I was frustrated to be dealing with Candida again. I was irritated that I've had such a long struggle with my immune and digestive systems. And I was annoyed that I had to go back to the Candida diet and probiotics to rid myself of this stuff.

Susanna smiled and said the anger and emotion were coming from the deeper breathing in my yoga. The deep breathing was getting to old stored energy. It was releasing some of the anger I had tucked deep inside.

Susanna saw two Lori's. One was the "Working Lori": strong, professional, "perfect me"—my masculine energy. The other Lori is where most of my feminine energy was. This was where I swept all my emotions under the rug. Her goal was to blend the two Lori's. That would be divine!

We talked about why old behaviors continued even though they were less intense now. Susanna shared a great visual picture of how our energy loops like a spiral coil and as we grow and become more enlightened, the loop gets smaller. Each time we circle around and reach the same frequency where that behavior was in the past, we experience it again, although with less force. Okay, that made sense...but still I was tired of these behaviors already.

I got strong encouragement that day that I was almost "there." I was just under the surface about to break through, and I would soon see a significant change.

I left on cloud ten. I had a spiritual guide/teacher. The fact that I could acknowledge and identify with this was astounding! I felt so lifted up, so centered, so loved by the universe.

I noticed people noticing me. As I walked by, people turned and smiled. My heart chakra was opening and people were seeing my inner beauty. I was *sharing* my inner self with others and felt wonderful to be alive.

⎈ ⎈ ⎈

At first my yoga classes, like anything, were a bit intimidating. Learning some Korean words and customs, and learning the new stretching moves. I experienced a lot of soreness in my solar plexus (third chakra). The headmaster told me this was caused by blocked energy and would pass. By the third class my entire abdomen hurt; after my fourth class I felt great...and noticed I hadn't had a craving for wine all week. Wow!

By the end of the second week I saw huge changes. *No* cravings for wine or sugar. I was sleeping like a baby, felt centered and connected. I had a whole new feeling of calm. My stomach wasn't bloated and my baggy clothes felt looser. For New Year's Eve I didn't even care if I drank—*that* was a first!

I went for my massage after one week of yoga and my massage therapist said, "Your spine has spring to it and your lymph system is completely cleaned out."

He couldn't believe what happened in just one week. He was impressed. He knew all about my issues and how frustrated I had been since we first met in July when I had felt my worst. He reminded me about the healing properties of blueberries (high antioxidants). His wife ate them every day for a year to help her recover from Candida.

Two weeks after starting yoga, I saw Susanna. She noticed the difference in my energy from the moment I walked through the door. We talked about why there was a difference in me doing aerobics vs. yoga. She said with aerobics I was using my will vs. yoga, which was connecting me with my emotions. With aerobics I felt in control. With yoga I felt calm, centered, spiritually connected. And, without the aerobics, I wasn't gaining weight, who would have thought?

I wasn't focused on my weight now and the healing came from within. I had found a whole new me—and was able to more fully forgive myself because of the compassion I was developing with yoga, acupuncture and energy healing. It was *finally* all coming together.

I lost weight every week. Some of my clothes started to fit! Including some clothes I had bought the year before but had never worn because of my weight gain.

I set a goal on January 1 to be in all my clothes by February 1. This time it felt possible because of the yoga. As February drew closer I was ecstatic to find that my stomach was flat—no bloating! And more clothes fit.

I ate blueberries, lots of fresh vegetables, quality grains (quinoa, millet, brown rice), made homemade bean-based soups and drank a green smoothie every day. I lifted weights and did yoga each three times a week. That's it. The weight thing was just happening. I wasn't focused on it, wasn't having to control anything and didn't have to monitor my every move.

Finally—what I always believed was possible was happening. I knew if I could quit the binges my body would just return to its natural size. My body became healthier day after day and I got smaller day by day, all without conscious effort.

After three weeks of yoga my lower back was more flexible than it had *ever* been. In three weeks! I had tried numerous times to do stretching routines to increase my flexibility, but it was minimal improvement at best. Now for the first time in my life, with legs extended on the floor, I was able reach down and touch my toes with my knees straight!

At my next massage my therapist said the Candida was gone. He could tell from the change in the texture of my skin on my hands. I felt so much better, the chronic itchy skin in my pelvis was gone and my head was clearer.

On February 1 I got on the scale just to see where I was. I weighed 116! I had lost 8 pounds in five weeks of yoga—at my height, that is phenomenal! I was in all of my clothes, I had reached my goal and I felt incredible. It had happened so quickly once I removed the blocked energy.

I still had 4 pounds to lose to get back to where I was post-EAS and make my smallest outfits comfortable, but I knew it would come. The important thing was, now I could open my closet, pull out anything and wear it again. Whew! I was psyched, but this time the level of enthusiasm I experienced came from a place of peace and inner knowing.

Henry

So that left one thing, Henry. After my first week of yoga, one day when we were talking I noticed his eyes—the way I used to. I noticed the warmth and beauty of his big brown eyes and how lovingly he looked at me. It was a start.

As the next couple of weeks passed I felt myself opening to Henry. I was more genuinely interested in him and what he was doing. He spent some time with Susanna's husband Satish, an energy healer, who suggested he do a ten-day master cleanse to gain clarity about his life.

Satish reminded Henry of the path he was on long before I came into the picture and gave him inspiration and a level of positivity I hadn't seen since we had been together. Wow—could this actually be happening?

It continued. We started to talk more and laugh some. We held hands as we fell asleep at night. I was back being a clown like the old days. Jumping unexpectedly into his arms when he left for work, or giving a "TV kiss."

The "TV kiss" is a term my sister Keri coined when she was four years old. Mom watched the soap *Search for Tomorrow,* and Keri would give Mom a "TV kiss," which was moving her head side to side many times in feigned passion!

For a while I thought I could get back the passion I had for Henry and fall in love again. The fact that I was able to re-engage with him at all was very unlike me. Once I'm done with a relationship, it's over. Although I tried my feelings faded in and out. I couldn't find where I lost him.

From my perspective things weren't changing. He was still in his own world trying to find his ignition switch and I was tired of feeling alone. We pleasantly coexisted and each did our own thing. I got back into golfing and made new friends. We were heading into year six of me carrying the financial burden.

Over time we had evolved into good friends.

There was no anger, no resentment and I was able to fully see the value of our relationship, but the universe started speaking to me—loudly! It was time to end the cycle of "Lori the caretaker". I realized I went into the relationship ready to help "change" him from the person he was because I knew he had so much potential. I knew better than that. I grew a lot before I connected with Henry, but not enough to keep myself out of the caretaker role.

The words to *It's Too Late Baby* were *so* fitting to our situation. I was glad for the experience and the love I shared with him, but the fire was gone.

ɤɤɤ

It was a difficult breakup. Henry felt it was a mistake and that we could find our way back to each other. And I needed my freedom from the situation. The change in his physical demeanor once he accepted the breakup was pronounced. Suddenly he was confident and determined. We agreed to remain friends and continue to write and record music together.

I went from a marriage where I was dominated, scared and abused to a relationship where I ran the show. Still not what I wanted, but with Henry I could see the good in our relationship. He opened my eyes, taught me new things and trusted me. Because of Henry, I grew.

Summary of Progress

✔ Through journaling I identified how significantly sugar affected my daily life, even though my diet is healthy (grains, fresh vegetables, tempeh, tofu and berries and avoiding high-sugar fruits and processed foods). I realized my pull to drink was tied to the resurgence of Candida and the sugar train; I wasn't fighting bulimia.

✔ I found a natural way to increase my protein intake by making raw green smoothies.

✔ My hormones were out of whack, which was contributing to my issues. I was in perimenopause.

✔ With my second energy healer I found a deeper spiritual connection, learned more about meditation and started to open my heart chakra and show my true self to others. I was connecting with my feminine energy and emotions.

✔ Through yoga and deep breathing I experienced a quantum leap in my healing and spiritual connection.

Chapter 17

Observations and Summary of Approach

Do not go where the path may lead, go instead where there is no path and leave a trail.
—Ralph Waldo Emerson

G rowing up in the medical community, I'd gotten a thorough understanding of the healthcare system. At age ten, I was exposed to mental illnesses of all types at the private psychiatric hospital my father ran.

All of us have memories that are deeply implanted, impressions from growing up. One day, when I was twelve, I watched a woman withdraw money from the business office at my dad's hospital. Her kneecaps were so skinny they looked as if her bones would break through the skin at any second. After she signed papers and withdrew her money, she immediately went to the bathroom. A few minutes later she emerged wiping her hands. I asked my dad about her and he told me she suffered from obsessive-compulsive disorder and was anorexic to boot. This disturbing sight made a huge impression on me.

People come and go from psych hospitals. Some don't get well.

As a kid, I wasn't convinced that "counseling" was the way to deal with these troubling emotional and mental illnesses. Growing up in a family woven with lots of hospital-speak about costs and insurance, I knew that people spent a *lot* of money on this type of treatment under the hospital umbrella. Surely, my young mind told me, there must be other options.

When I was older and worked in medical records I saw first-hand the implications of the cost of treatment and what happened when insurance stopped paying.

I tried counseling in '85 to see if I was bulimic. But, after nine months of counseling, I still didn't have a clue how to fix it. No one along "the healing path" ever talked about learning to feel emotions.

So I kept searching for my path. My real journey began after I stopped counseling. I didn't want to pour thousands of dollars out to counselors in search of my cure. If there was going to be a cure, it was going to be one that I fully participated in. I wanted *my* answers, not something someone suggested to me in a counseling session. I needed to really believe in it.

Insurance coverage is limited and forces families to pay significant out-of-pocket costs. This results in huge financial stress at a time when their loved one may be fighting a life or death battle.

People suffering with eating disorders are often re-hospitalized—this approach isn't working!

The costs of eating disorders rise far above the treatments. They include lost productivity, missed work and poor performance, not to mention the effects on the family unit. Whether it is a young child or an adult trying to function in the role of family provider the disruption can be devastating. And the person with the eating disorder misses out on years of his or her life, *obsessed* about something that, in the end, really doesn't rank all that high on the list of life's priorities.

We spend our lives so worried about what other people think of us—only to find out, other people aren't even thinking about us! They are busy with their lives and issues. We are all "extras" in everyone else's movies. We missed the boat—the love and acceptance we are looking for needs to come from within. *We need to love and accept ourselves.*

It's More than Mental Health

To fully understand and recover from an eating disorder we have to address more than the emotional issues. Many times the root cause can include chemical issues or deficiencies that feed the symptoms. By ignoring these, the problems will persist. Since eating disorders are considered a mental illness many treatment plans only address the emotional aspects.

Treatment must be broader because of the long-term effects caused by the behaviors of bingeing, purging and starving your body. Something I can attest to—now that I am in my late forties, I have struggled to create balance in my life. The problems with my blood sugar and conditions created from bingeing were exacerbated by the Candida. I have to continually monitor the "sugar train" to avoid the pull to drink full bottles of wine in one sitting.

An Alternative Approach— Healing from Within

Healing from my eating disorder took finding the answers inside me to ease the pain and remove the blocked energy from my conditioning and perception of the world. I learned to express myself and to let go of control. I had the answers all along; I always knew I would find them. When I asked for the answers and expressed my desire to evolve, they were given to me. Sometimes my healing moved slower than I thought it should. But I always got what I needed right when I needed it.

I recommend a healing path that includes getting

in touch with and using your energy source to heal. Finding your personal power and learning what balance means for you. Empowering yourself to function as a valuable individual in the circle of life.

We *all* have value, we *all* have purpose, we are *all* beautiful—just the way we are. It's not about perfection, it's not about control. It *is* about the flow of energy, it *is* about being in *this* moment, enjoying each and every day. It's about "wholeness." Finding the right station to tune in to and get the information you need, right now, *today,* to begin your path of healing.

I missed so much of my life waiting until I lost weight, waiting until I looked better, waiting until I felt better about myself, waiting until...a forever that never came.

So let's recap.

The Key Non-psychological Contributors to My Bulimia

Earlier I covered the psychological issues that contributed to my bulimia. Many of which are well documented as typical causes of an eating disorder. But I believe there were a number of other factors that contributed to and intensified my eating disorder, which is why I struggled with it for so many years. Things that were more chemical or caused by my "conditioning," these were:

⟡ Heavy use of antibiotics in my school years
⟡ Vegetarian diet—not getting enough tryptophan to create essential amino acids for proper brain "mood" function
⟡ Sugar sensitivity
⟡ Candida
⟡ Low-fat diet—no enough oil and "healthy fat"

Key Steps to My Healing

Here are the key steps I followed to find my healing and create a balanced, centered, grounded human being.

⟡ Improved my self-esteem:
  • Repeated positive affirmations
  • Changed my circle of friends from negative to positive influences
  • Pushed myself out of my comfort zone to try new things
  • Found a creative outlet that helped me learn how to do things without "being in control"
⟡ Used the power of my subconscious:
  • Set and achieved goals, which improved my self-confidence

- Used my intention to create the body and life I wanted
- Used *feelings* and visualization to manifest results I wanted

✧ Improved nutrition:
- Made a commitment to my health with EAS Body-*for*-LIFE eating and exercise plan
- Used natural supplements to improve physical issues created by my eating disorder and vegetarian diet
- Used journaling to create awareness of the effects of sugar on my system and identify patterns that created binges with food or alcohol (a.k.a. the sugar train)

✧ Improved physical and mental health with bodywork:
- Completed Hellerwork treatment series— to learn about my relationship with my body and transform it
- Received acupuncture treatments—to leverage a natural proven method of treatment to improve my immune system, liver, kidney and spleen function (and reduce Candida and menopause symptoms)
- Practiced meditation
  - To quiet and balance my brain
  - To learn to be more conscious—in the moment

- To alleviate stress
- To create calm and balance in my life
- Which ultimately resulted in a connection with my spiritual dimension
- Received energy healing sessions
  - To enable my self-healing through the human energy field
  - To remove the long-held energies of my bulimia in my body
  - To gain a deeper understanding of causes and effects of my life experiences
  - To find a connection with myself
  - To forgive myself
  - To learn to love and accept myself
- Practiced yoga
  - To support my immune system
  - To increase my core strength
  - To gain additional healing through deep breathing
  - To further the fruits of my meditation
  - To exercise connected to my emotions vs. my will

Summary

This path to healing using my own power and inner guidance to create a better life and a healthy "Lori" cost me far less than what most people spend on clinical treatment and psychological counseling. Most of what I did wasn't covered by insurance, except for the counseling I did in '85. I was never "locked in" to any treatment plan or held hostage by what my insurance would or wouldn't pay. I controlled whom I saw and, when it didn't work, looked for another answer. I followed my gut and intuition—it never let me down.

My life is so incredibly different today than it was even three years ago. Through this process I watched as my personality and life began to unfold with a whole new focus and I saw the metamorphosis of my identification with myself from "a person with bulimia" to "a person."

So What Can You Do?

There is no one treatment plan for everyone. We are all on our own path. As you can see I tried many things and had to make my own decisions about what worked and what wasn't working for me. Determining where you are in your journey will help you to identify where to start.

Below I have listed the five key areas I addressed on my path to recovery. Read through each area and evaluate which areas you feel strong in and which areas you need to improve. Be honest with yourself! As you read this list listen to your inner guidance (your gut reaction). What specific items call out to you? Start there.

Come back and read the list again as you make improvements. Your inner guidance will lead you and will get stronger the more you listen and trust in it.

If you are struggling with food or alcohol, prioritize the nutrition and supplements (do you have a sugar train?) and bodywork. Through energy healing you can address self-esteem, identify and understand the causes and begin to heal. Then you can explore the power of your subconscious, which will enrich your life.

Five Key Areas for Study and Improvement:

1. Improve your self-esteem—there are many methods to do this. I feel it can be done most effectively through energy healing. See the resources section for more information.
2. Identify and understand the causes of your obsessive/addictive behavior or eating disorder—this can also be done through energy healing.

3. Embrace the power of your subconscious.
   - Buy the *What the Bleep Do We Know!?* DVD and watch it—more than once!
   - Study books by Jack Canfield, Napoleon Hill, Brian Tracy, Bill Harris, Dr. Wayne Dyer, Esther and Jerry Hicks and Lynn Grabhorn. See resources section for book list.
   - Watch *The Secret* DVD.
   - Learn to let everything be okay.
   - Let go of being perfect and negative self-talk.
   - Stop beating yourself up.
4. Nutrition and supplements
   - Read *The Schwarzbein Principle II* to learn about healing your metabolism.
   - Read *The Mood Cure* to learn about your emotional/brain health.
   - Read *Potatoes Not Prozac* to learn about sugar sensitivity.
   - Start journaling to identify patterns in your eating habits.
   - If you are unsure of your level of "nutrition health," find a holistic nutritionist, naturopath or integrative therapist to work with.
   - Eat 5 to 6 small meals a day with carbohydrates and protein at every meal.
   - Eat 3 to 5 servings of vegetables everyday.

- Eat 1 to 2 servings of fruit everyday. If you are sugar-sensitive, limit this to berries, which are lower in sugar.
- Eat at least one serving of green leafy vegetables every day.
- Try a green smoothie! Read *Green For Life.*
- Drink water 6 to 8 glasses every day— stay hydrated.
- Test your zinc level with liquid zinc available at most health food stores. If needed, use zinc supplement. Retest occasionally to maintain the appropriate level of zinc your body needs.
- Take vitamin C, start with 500 mg to improve your adrenal function and support the process of amino acid conversion for proper brain function.
- Take vitamin B complex, 50 mg, to help your body break down carbohydrates as food.
- If you are sugar sensitive *always* carry a snack with you. A protein bar or a few almonds and some dried fruit, or raw vegetables and nuts. Don't go more than three hours between meals. This makes it much easier to control cravings.

5. Improve your physical and mental health with bodywork.
   - Hellerwork—consider taking a series of sessions.
   - Energy healing—find an energy healer to work with—this is critical to your success! If there is no one where you live, you can work long distance with a healer. See the resources section for more information.
   - Acupuncture—visit with a reputable acupuncture practitioner. To determine where your body is lacking (liver, kidney or spleen function, chi energy, yin/yang, immune system or other areas).
   - Meditation—take time daily to sit and meditate.
     - Purchase guided meditations if you are new to meditation.
     - Purchase meditation music and listen to it to help you relax.
     - Learn to tune in and listen to your inner guidance.
     - Better yet, meditate with Holosync.
   - Yoga—another critical element to success
     - Find a yoga class you can attend 3 to 4 times a week.
     - Look for yoga that focuses on combined elements of breathing and stretching.

- The oxygen from the deep breathing will provide much needed healing.
- Avoid "hot yoga" as this will stress an already weakened immune system!
- Exercise
  - Include both weight training and cardio into your fitness routine. Weight training will tighten your muscles, give you more shape, help you burn fat, build muscle and is great prevention for osteoporosis.
  - Purchase the Body-*for*-LIFE book and do a challenge.
  - Consider working with a personal trainer. Carefully select someone who will understand your situation and provide a positive and supportive approach to your fitness plan. You don't need a drill sergeant!
  - If you can't afford a personal trainer check your local bookstore or Amazon.com for books and tapes by Kathy Smith. She has created a lot of effective workouts in many flavors.

ಖಿ ಖಿ ಖಿ

For additional assistance or information you can contact me directly Lori@Lori-Hanson.com.

Chapter 18

Riding the Waves

The best thing about tomorrow is
that I can be better than I am today.
—Tiger Woods

I spent over thirty years of my life obsessed with how I looked in the mirror and what other people thought of me. More than thirty years with low self-esteem and a poor self-image! I had flashes of brilliance and accomplishments, but wasn't able to allow myself to own it or believe I was really worth anything.

I was *so* focused on figuring out how to measure up that I let most of my life slip past me while I worked myself to exhaustion only to lay on the couch in a food-induced coma or drunken stupor. I kept waiting until *this* happened or *that* happened and my life would be perfect. Perfect? What is *that*?

I was committed from an early age to growing and evolving as a person. So I continued to look for answers, new ways to help me improve my self-worth and find a big slice of self-esteem. An avid sports fan, I loved watching my favorites—Michael Jordan, Dale Earnhardt, Andre Agassi and Tiger Woods compete. I loved their spirit, their confidence and their "Never give up" attitude. I wanted *that* kind of confidence in myself.

Healing Is a Journey Not a Destination

As I started healing my energy I had to accept that I was on a journey. Life isn't a destination. For years, I wanted so badly to get to that point where life would be the way I wanted it to be. I would have the perfect body, make millions of dollars, live in a large house with a big yard, and be wildly success-ful. I *knew* that was the life I was supposed to have. I set goals each year toward making it happen! The timing just hadn't come together yet.

The concept of "spiritual" eluded me for many years and I never thought I would find any kind of spiritual connection. I lived in a two-dimensional world with mind and body. I left the spiritual for the weak, those who needed something to believe in. I didn't—I was strong and I could handle everything life threw at me.

From the first energy healing session I learned how much I was missing by:

✧ Living my life armored in my masculine energy
✧ How stressed and exhausted my body was because I never let my guard down
✧ How much I was affecting my outcomes in life by being competitive with men and feeling no connection with women
✧ How much I could gain by learning to use my feminine energy
✧ The connection I could make with people by using all of my gifts as a human being

I wondered why it had taken me so long to come to this point of awakening. Why did I have to suffer with bulimia for so many years? Why couldn't I have the control other people had? Why was this *my* journey? What was the point?

The first time Anne Rojo told me about how our bodies are designed to heal themselves, I believed it. The more work I did to increase my flow of energy and release the energy blocks I carried inside for so many years, the more I became an example of this.

Then, a couple of years into the alternative work I was doing I started thinking about writing this book. Telling my life story and the path I found to heal myself.

Stepping Outside the Box: Alternative Healing Path

My path has been such a contrast from my up-bringing, growing up in the health-care arena. Hell, going to a chiropractor in the '80s, it was scandalous! But throughout my adult life, I always believed people should be as self-sufficient as they can. I've never been dependent on other people. To me it was learning how to:

⬧ Leverage what *you* know, the answers you have inside.

⬧ Follow what *your* experience tells you.

That's why all of the energy healing, acupuncture and yoga made so much sense to me.

Trusting Your Gut

What's frustrating is that it took me so long to find out about things that have been in existence for thousands of years in other cultures. In Western culture modern-day medicine and prescription drugs are the answer to everything. (Ever notice how many TV and radio commercials are for prescription drugs?) Bullshit! In Western culture businesses make money when people are sick. And so many people don't even ask questions. They just follow what their health practitioner tells them. Most people aren't in touch with their inner guidance enough to trust their gut and question if what they are being told *feels* right.

When I consulted my OB-GYN of fourteen years about getting some blood work done to check my hormone and thyroid levels for my integrative therapy work, he gave me a "there, there" attitude and said I shouldn't believe everything I read on the Internet. It's my body! I never went to see him again.

What we believe so strongly influences our health, and healing. Recent best-selling books like *The Secret* by Rhonda Byrne show how critical positive thoughts and a positive environment are to aid in recovery.

Connection with Self

There are many alternative methods to find healing. Alternative isn't bad, insurance just doesn't pay for it! The irony is that many dis-eases are caused by the lack of connection with self. We are so busy doing, going and running—we never stop to listen to our inner guidance. *Each of us has the tools we need to heal inside.* But to truly heal, we must learn to be still, to be comfortable "just being" without outside distractions, to listen and to connect with our spirit.

Susanna recently shared a great analogy with me. If we use meditation to get in touch with our inner guidance or our higher self, the connection and guidance we get from our meditation is like having a helicopter to view the labyrinth of life. (Like being the witness.) It gives us an aerial view so we can keep ourselves on the right path. It keeps us from getting stuck in the wrong area or the maze.

Family Relationships Today

My relationship with my family ebbs and flows. I'm closest with my brother as we are very like-minded in business, work ethic and determination. We can share so much with each other. He has four beautiful children that I am close to and miss dearly since moving to California.

I talk with my sisters on occasion and recently found a connection with my oldest sister and have developed a friendship with her. But I wouldn't describe these relationships as close.

I enjoy golfing with my parents, and am grateful to my mother for teaching me sewing and cooking skills at an early age. I found ways to identify with her and enjoy her company as I've gotten older. My father continues to be a great place to get advice and I still look up to him. He had a great career and was a visionary in the health-care field.

A Sense of Self

I didn't grow up with a strong sense of self. I didn't feel I was important or that what I was interested in as a young child mattered. Our schedule revolved around Mom's work schedule. I know children whose mothers were home with them when they were young. Their mothers took time to read to them or take them to the zoo or the museum— things that made them feel important as a youngster. To me this is a strong link in creating self-esteem and a strong sense of self.

What I see looking back is that my parents were both working hard to get their needs met, to fill their voids, to feel like *they* measured up. Neither of them did anything to intentionally hurt me. And although our views in life are not the same I know they love me and I love them. In the end, they were great parents. I picked them!

My mother contacted me recently after some reading she did helped her understand the impact of the instability of my upbringing. She realizes now that I didn't feel important to her and that because she was "really into her personal music ego" she didn't appreciate her role as a mother. The connection she feels with her latest grandchild and great grandchildren has helped her realize all the things she missed when we were kids. This is a conversation I never thought I would have! I let go a long time ago, but to have her finally "get it" felt really good. Little Lori was giggling with delight after this conversation.

My Path

In the last year, I've come to terms with the fact that this *is* my path. It wasn't the wrong path. Everything in life plays a part in fulfilling life's purpose. I *have* felt a shift in what I feel my life's purpose is. I've worked in corporate America for twenty-six years and have seen so many people pushing themselves like I did, or worse. So many people missing the point—like I did. *It's not about how hard we work, it's about finding out what our true life's purpose is and connecting with it.*

"Nothing exists without a purpose to bring it into being and that purpose calls until we respond. And when we do respond to the call of the purpose, we enter into a sacred dance with Life."[1] I found this in an awesome book called *You Are The Answer*, by Michael Tamura.

Michael's book is something I couldn't have read two years ago. It was too "out there" for me. But as I have traveled my path to healing, some of my beliefs have changed and I now embrace myself and the spiritual journey I have for this life. Michael says that spiritual growth is the purpose of fulfilling our life's purpose. "To be who we are, to have all that is within us and to fully express our divine heritage— that is our purpose for living and the destination of our journey."[2]

It wasn't about my body, or what other people thought about me. But it *was* about my finding and opening up my personal power center. By engaging my power center my interactions with people *feel* more genuine. I feel a deeper warmth in my interactions with others. I can tell I give off a different vibe than I used to, based on how people respond to me. I feel as an individual I truly have something to share with others, something important. I have value and meaning! And little ole rebellious me has found a connection to the spiritual path in this life.

Full Circle

The lyrics for the chorus of *Up Above the Clouds* came to me over a year before I finished the book. When I started to hear the melody and lyrics I knew this song was about coming full circle, about my healing. The verses came to me the month I finished this book.

Up Above the Clouds

I'm up above the clouds
Now I see the light
It took so long
But I had to get it right

Spent most of my life
The other side of the line
Felt like my life
Was a waste of time
Up one day, and down the next
I tell ya my life
Was one big mess

One day through the rain
I caught a glimpse of the sun
Knew my life
Had just begun
Got a taste of happiness
Changed my direction
And found success

Now I'm up above the clouds
Now I see the light
It took so long
But I had to get it right

Way up here above the clouds
I'm so high I won't come down

I found freedom
Without control
Life is peaceful
I am whole
Energy just has to flow
My life has meaning
Now that I know

Now I'm up above the clouds
Now I see the light
It took so long
But I had to get it right

Now I'm up above the clouds
Now I see the light
It took so long
But I finally got it right

Lyrics by Lori Hanson, © Shewolf Music

A Balanced Life

I am well. My life now has balance, patience, happiness and even bliss on occasion. I believe the results I ask for from the universe will come—when they are supposed to. I'm getting better about not being so attached to the outcomes in life, to "let everything be okay." I don't get so rattled when someone at work does something dumb, or plays political games.

I now understand that life is a journey and there will always be opportunities that will bring growth if I'm open to them. I'm learning to ride the waves of life, which aren't nearly as high as they used to be. And most of all, I am learning to enjoy life without my compulsive behaviors to drink or binge.

I'm learning how to live life as one blended person—and not ignore Little Lori. I prioritize golf because I realized it was Little Lori calling. She loves being outside soaking up the sunshine and playing. I take the dogs to the ocean because it's Little Lori who loves the sound of the waves and playing with the dogs in the water. I make a conscious effort to be playful with Henry and not to take life so seriously.

I'm living life in the present, enjoying each and every day, stopping to smell the roses and passing by mirrors without even looking. I truly love my body and myself more and more each day. And from that place, the love I give myself—without anyone else's approval—I have found complete peace and freedom. I have found my path.

Resources

Recommended Books/Audio Series

Many of the authors listed here have multiple books and audio series available on their websites. I've just listed a few here.

Victoria Boutenko, www.RawFamily.com
* ✧ *Green for Life*

Barbara Ann Brennan, www.BarbaraBrennan.com
* ✧ *Hands Of Light, A Guide to Healing Through the Human Energy Field*

Jack Canfield, www.JackCanfield.com
* ✧ *The Success Principles, The Power of Focus, The Aladdin Factor*

James L. Crabtree, www.CoreStarEnergyHealing.com
* ✧ *The Seven Windows to Wholeness*

Wiliam G. Crook
* ✧ *The Yeast Connection, A Medical Breakthrough*

Kathleen Des Maisons. www.Amazon.com
* ✧ *Potatoes Not Prozac*

Dr. Wayne Dyer, www.DrWayneDyer.com
* ✧ *The Power Of Intention, Being in Balance*

Lynn Grabhorn, www.LynnGrabhorn.com
* ✧ *Excuse Me Your Life is Waiting*

Esther and Daniel Hicks, www.Abraham-Hicks.com
  ✧ *Ask and It Is Given: Learning to Manifest Your Desires*
Bill Harris, www.Amazon.com
  ✧ *Thresholds of the Mind*
Napoleon Hill, www.Amazon.com
  ✧ *Keys to Success: The 17 Principles of Personal Achievement*
Napoleon Hill, W. Clement Stone www.Amazon.com
  ✧ *Success Through A Positive Mental Attitude*
Christiane Northrup
  ✧ *Women's Bodies, Women's Wisdom: Creating Physical and Emotional Health and Healing*
Bill Phillips and Phil D'Orso, www.BodyForLife.com
  ✧ *Body-for-LIFE, 12 Weeks to Mental and Physical Strength*
Julia Ross, www.TheMoodCure.com
  ✧ *The Diet Cure*
  ✧ *The Mood Cure*
Diane Schwarzbein, www.SchwarzbeinPrinciple.com
  ✧ *The Schwarzbein Principle II*
Michael J. Tamura
  ✧ *You Are The Answer*
Brian Tracy, www.BrianTracy.com
  ✧ *The Psychology of Achievement, The Science of Self-Confidence*

Acupuncture Consultations

  ✧ Contact Susanna Horton in Los Angeles, through her website: www.InnerCosmos.com.
  ✧ Contact Shauna Sindo, ShaunaSindo@yahoo.com, or (928) 202-8670.

Candida Remedies

- ✧ Follow a Candida Diet (www.arthritistrust.org/
  Books/The Art of Getting Well)*
- ✧ Quick Candida Cleanse by Zand (available at
  Whole Foods or check online for suppliers)*
- ✧ Acidophilus Pearls (probiotics available at
  local health food stores or check online for
  suppliers)*
- ✧ Eat blueberries daily for 6 to 12 months for a great
  natural dose of antioxidants
- ✧ Contact Ann Boroch, Naturopath and Certified
  Nutritional Consultant, who practices in
  Studio City, California through her website:
  www.AnnBoroch.com. Ann specializes in Candida
  and many other health issues.

Energy Healers

- ✧ Contact Tina Meyer, who practices in Denver,
  Colorado. Her e-mail is: Info@InBodyment.org,
  phone (720) 840-5397. Or visit her website:
  www.InBodyment.com.
- ✧ Contact Susanna Horton, who practices in Los Angeles,
  through her website: www.InnerCosmos.com.
- ✧ www.CoreStarEnergyHealing.com – This site lists
  graduates by state.
- ✧ www.BarbaraBrennan.com – This site lists graduates
  by state.

---

*The amount of time to follow the diet and take supplements depends on
the severity and length of time you have been fighting with Candida.

Resources

Feng Shui Consultation

✧ Contact Elaine Giftos Wright. Her e-mail is:
egwright@way2fengshui.com, phone (800) 947-
7756. Or visit her website: www.Way2FengShui.com.

Hellerwork

✧ In Denver, contact Anne Rojo. Her e-mail is:
info@AnneRojo.com, phone (303) 442-8424.
✧ Visit www.Hellerwork.com to find a practitioner in
your area.

Meditation

✧ Visit www.Centerpointe.com to learn more about
Holosync meditation.

Methods to Improve Self-esteem

✧ Check www.JackCanfield.com for the *Self-esteem
and Peak Performance* or *Maximum Confidence*
audio series by Jack Canfield.
✧ www.Amazon.com has a wide variety of books on
self-esteem.
✧ Find a personal coach who works with self-esteem.
Check the Internet for resources.
✧ Will Matthews is an acquaintance from Denver. He
offers coaching through his website:
www.SecondWindPerformance.com.
✧ Jack Canfield offers personal coaching through his
website: www.JackCanfield.com.

Yoga

With yoga you have many options! Choose one that focuses on deep breathing and healing. I would recommend finding a yoga class that is based on authenticity vs. the latest trend.

⬥ www.Dahn.yoga offers classes nationally. Their classes are a combination of stretching and deep breathing. Their approach is much like joining a gym and you have to pay up front. Sign up for a month and see if you feel a difference. You can always use the CD practice at home if this method is price-prohibitive.

Additional books are on the way including cookbooks! For more information about upcoming books please visit my website: www.Lori-Hanson.com, or feel free to contact me directly: Lori@Lori-Hanson.com.

Notes

Introduction

1. The Center for Counseling and Health Resources, Inc., "Eating Disorders," http://www.aplaceofhope.com/more_eating.html (accessed May 17, 2007).

2. PsychCentral, "Eating Disorders Cost Millions of Dollars for Many U.S. Businesses," http://psychcentral.com/blog/archives/2004/08/17/eating-disorders-cost-millions-of-dollars-for-many-us-businesses (accessed May 16, 2007).

3. Shaefer, Gayla, *FloridaToday.com*, "Eating Disorders Stretch Beyond Stereotypes," January 16, 2006. *http://members.aol.com/brevardanad/FT012006.html* (accessed May 25, 2007).

Chapter 1

1. Sacker and Buff, *Regaining Your Self*, 19.

Chapter 10

1. http://www.hellerwork.com/ (accessed November 12, 2005).

2. DesMaisons, *Potatoes Not Prozac*, 22-23.

3. Ibid., 119.

4. http://www.holistichorizons.com/

Chapter 11

1. *The Yeast Connection*, "About Candida Yeast," http://www.yeastconnection.com/about_can_yeast.html (accessed April 21, 2007).
2. Schwarzbein, *The Schwarzbein Principle II*, 431.
3. Ibid., 432.
4. Ross, *The Mood Cure*, 5.
5. Ibid., 8.
6. Ibid., 10.
7. Ibid.

Chapter 12

1. Holosync: Centerpointe Research Institute, http://www.centerpointe.com/ (accessed November 12, 2005).
2. Ibid.
3. Ibid.
4. Harris, *A Personal Message to You* (a pamphlet that came with the CDs).
5. Harris, *Thresholds of the Mind*, 84.

Chapter 13

1. Hicks, *Ask and It Is Given,* 15.
2. Ibid.
3. Ibid., 144.

Chapter 16

1. Boutenko, *Green For Life*, 47.

Chapter 18

1. Tamura, *You Are the Answer*, 1.
2. Ibid., 5.

Bibliography

Banks, C. Tillery, *Hello to Me With Love: Poems of Self-Discovery*, William Morrow & Co., 1987.

Boutenko, Victoria, *Green For Life*, Ashland: Raw Family Publishing, 2005.

Canfield, Jack, *Self-Esteem and Peak Performance* (audiotapes). Boulder: CareerTrack Publications, 1987

DesMaisons, Kathleen, Ph.D., *Potatoes Not Prozac*, New York: Fireside, 1998.

Harris, Bill, *A Personal Message to You* (pamphlet), The Holosync Solution.

Harris, Bill, *Thresholds of the Mind*, Beaverton: Centerpointe Press, 2002.

Hicks, Esther and Jerry, *Ask and It Is Given, Learning To Manifest Your Desires*, Carlsbad: Hay House, Inc., 2004.

Ross, Julia, M.A., *The Mood Cure*, New York: Penguin Group, 2002.

Sacker, Ira M., M.D. and Sheila Buff, *Regaining Your Self*, New York: Hyperion, 2007.

Schwarzbein, Diana, M.D., *The Schwarzbein Principle II*, Deerfield Beach: Health Communications, Inc., 2002.

Tamura, Michael J., *You Are the Answer*, Mt. Shasta: Star of Peace Publishing, 2002.

What the Bleep Do We Know!? DVD, directed by Mark Vicente, Betsy Chasse, William Arntz, 20th Century Fox, 2005.

Lyrics

For more information about upcoming Shewolf CDs
and additional books please visit my website:
www.Lori-Hanson.com,
or feel free to contact me directly:
Lori@Lori-Hanson.com.

Index

Index

Did You Borrow This Copy?

To order this book by
Shewolf Press

Online orders:
www.ShewolfPress.com

E-mail:
Lori@Lori-Hanson.com

Postal orders:
Shewolf Press
25379 Wayne Mills Pl. #228
Valencia, CA 91355
661-670-0729

Please send [   ] copies of *It Started With Pop-Tarts...* @ $15.95

Shipping and handling: $5.00 for the first book and $1.00 for each additional

Payment: Certified check or money order

Total $ _____

Name: _____
Address: _____
City: _____ State: _____ Zip: _____
Telephone: _____
E-mail address: _____

Wholesale discounts available on large quantities.

Thank you!